THE UNITED STATES
AND THE GLOBAL ECONOMY
SINCE 1945

HARBRACE
BOOKS
ON AMERICA

SINCE 1945

THE UNITED STATES AND THE GLOBAL ECONOMY SINCE 1945

Henry C. Dethloff

Texas A & M University

Under the general editorship of

Gerald D. Nash

and

Richard W. Etulain

University of New Mexico

Harcourt Brace College Publishers

Fort Worth   Philadelphia   San Diego   New York   Orlando   Austin   San Antonio
Toronto   Montreal   London   Sydney   Tokyo

Publisher	Christopher P. Klein
Senior Acquisitions Editor	David C. Tatom
Developmental Editor	J. Claire Brantley
Project Editor	Betsy Cummings
Production Manager	Lois West
Art Director	Garry Harman
Picture Editor	Carrie Ward
Photo Researcher	Lili Weiner
Cover image	© Rob Day/SIS

Harcourt Brace College Publishers may provide complimentary instructional aids and supplements or supplement packages to those adopters qualified under our adoption policy. Please contact your sales representative for more information. If as an adopter or potential user you receive supplements you do not need, please return to your sales representative or send them to:

Attn: Returns Department
Troy Warehouse
465 South Lincoln Drive
Troy, MO 63379

Address for Editorial Correspondence: Harcourt Brace College Publishers, 301 Commerce Street, Suite 3700, Fort Worth, TX 76102.

Address for Orders: Harcourt Brace & Company, 6277 Sea Harbor Drive, Orlando, FL 32887-6777. 1-800-782-4479, or 1-800-433-0001 (in Florida).

Library of Congress Catalog Card Number: 96-78584

ISBN: 0-15-502854-5

Printed in the United States of America

6 8 9 0 1 2 3 4 5 067 0 9 8 7 6 5 4 3 2 1

PREFACE

History is the story of change. This book is a brief introduction to economic changes of a truly global dimension. The world which we have spoken and written about for the past ten thousand years has taken on yet another new conformation. We now have a picture of it. The photograph of Earth taken during the flight of Apollo 17 in December 1972, is one of the world's most published photographs. As Donald (Deke) K. Slayton, director of the Apollo Flight Crew Operations observed, "almost every astronaut and cosmonaut who circled planet Earth has observed from orbit there are no national borders visible on this beautiful globe." National boundaries and history as we know it really seem less applicable in this new global perspective. While researching and writing a book on the history of the NASA Johnson Space Center (*Suddenly, Tomorrow Came. . . A History of Johnson Space Center*, NASA, 1993), one of the things that struck me most strongly was that this world has become a far different place than it was before the advent of human space flight. Lyndon Baines Johnson may have been correct when he observed in 1957 that with Sputnik "a new era of history dawned over the world."

Since World War II, the world has become a much more homogenous, interrelated, and integrated place. The United States had much to do with changing that world. Through much of the past half-century, the United States has "Americanized" the global economy; and, U.S. businesses and consumers have been adjusting to the new realities of the global economy for which they are in large measure responsible. The U.S. economy and our perception of history and the world is being globalized. To think globally is to put aside the "flat-earth" nation-state kind of thinking and see things from a different perspective.

Globalization, the multinational corporation, and the development of a global economy confounds the past five centuries of historical development in which the underlying theme has been the rise of the nation-state and the development of the national economy. It confronts in particular the American's sense of historic isolation, independence, and apartness. It is a more competitive, complex, and difficult world. The development of a global economy creates problems, particularly for Americans who have been the critical catalysts in its coming.

To be sure, Sputnik, space, and the U.S. Apollo flights are only a few of the many things that have contributed to a significant change over the past half-century in how we live and earn a living. World War II had a great impact on how we perceive the world and human affairs. The war was truly a global affair. Moreover, after the war ended, Americans, unlike in the aftermath of previous wars, remained involved in the world. The "boys" or Johnny, to paraphrase the old Civil War song, really did not come marching home again. From 1945 to date, U.S. soldiers have been present throughout much of the world. The Truman Doctrine and NATO committed the United States to a permanent global presence.

The Marshall Plan became a statement of U.S. policy dedicated to the proposition that no nation or peoples can truly remain secure or prosperous in a world of poverty and want. The Marshall Plan took the global view that human affairs and destinies were inextricably linked, and a single nation could not be isolated from that condition. The Marshall Plan had much to do with the creation of a global economy. It also subliminally if not overtly struck at the U.S. tradition of "splendid isolation."

A global view of history was inadvertently reinforced by the atomic bomb. Atomic warfare threatened not just a nation but humankind everywhere. Paradoxically, the Cold War itself may have helped construct a sense of globalism. Nations became interdependent militarily and politically. This, of course, has happened throughout history as different alliances and leagues were formed, but this time the alliances became more tightly constructed, financially and militarily. The USSR and NATO created hemispheric defense policies with important economic consequences. All the while the Marshall Plan and trade agreements created closer economic associations and interdependencies within the blocs.

While the U.S. and the U.S.S.R. divided most of the world's nations and its peoples into two military and economic blocs organized to confront each other, there was, to be sure, a more subtle, untested, but intrusive international association of nations that included the eastern and western blocs. The United Nations, for whatever else it may or may not have accomplished during its first half-century, contributed strongly to a rising global perspective on human affairs. The World Bank and General Agreements on Tariff and Trade have helped build global trade opportunities and associations. The greater movement and migration of peoples that has occurred since World War II has also, while creating new tensions, contributed to a new interconnectedness of peoples and nations. In addition, Americans in particular have developed a new global perspective simply because they spend more time abroad, either in the military or as businessmen and women, tourists, and travelers. They sense that the pulse of commerce in Hong Kong, Beijing, Tokyo, Paris, London, Amsterdam, Munich, Vienna, Budapest, Moscow, and the other great cities of the world resonates globally.

These conditions have provided the infrastructure and the incentive to developing global economy. Science, real time global communications systems, jet aircraft, and space flight have all contributed to the growth of global trade and commerce. The United States has been central to the creation of the global economy and in turn that globalization has begun to change the way we think, the way we earn a living, and the way we live.

A careful examination of this text provides a better understanding of the dynamics of U.S. history. It should help explain what has happened to U.S. businesses and consumers since World War II. Globalization has been the primary force affecting change in American life over the past half-century.

This book explores those factors that have been critical catalysts in the rise of the new global economy. It also seeks to provide a definition or characterization of that global economy. The world is neither now nor likely to become an open market place, conforming to an economist's model of a free market. Rather, what is being constructed appears to be a world of federated, regional economic systems, each somewhat autonomous, somewhat amorphous, and all somewhat interrelated. It is important that we understand the changes that are occurring in order that we might better cope, manage, and profit from those changes.

I should like to thank Gerald D. Nash and Richard Etulain who first invited me to prepare a volume of the Harcourt Brace "Contemporary America" series, then allowed me to shape that title in a way somewhat different than originally intended and then provided the counsel and careful editing to bring the work to a cogent close. Our association goes back a long time, and I was delighted to have the opportunity to renew it.

As always, I am grateful to my wife Myrtle Anne, for her constant support. In the past decade we have both had awakening to the global economy by virtue of a few trips abroad. To be sure, one does not have to go abroad to experience the global market place. Any business in any city of town will offer excellent instruction if one is observant.

I am grateful also to the editors and staff of Harcourt Brace who have so efficiently, expeditiously, and helpfully turned the raw manuscript into this readable, interesting, and informative introduction to what I truly believe may be a new and even more exciting era of history, a time when a global economy is being constructed and global interests and affairs begin to compete with the more traditional interests of nations and regions.

Henry C. Dethloff

CONTENTS

Part 1

THE AMERICANIZATION
OF THE WORLD ECONOMY
1945–1970

Chapter 1

THE LEGACY OF WAR

We live in a global economy. It is an economy and a world civilization built upon modern science and technology. Václav Havel, President of the Czech Republic, in an address in Philadelphia in July 1994, described ours as "the first civilization in the history of the human race that spans the entire globe and firmly binds together all human societies, submitting them to a common global destiny." It is a world phenomenon that is relatively new, but which has been in development for fully a half-century, and there are, of course, old if not ancient precedents. This new global economy and world civilization is newly formed, tenuous, perhaps transient, and certainly vulnerable to what Havel described as "chaos, disconnectedness and tribalism." It is also an economy and a world in which the United States is central.

Whereas the United States effectively withdrew from the world created by World War I and its aftermath and retreated even further during the Great Depression, since World War II the United States and the American people have remained very much a part of the world. America remained involved politically through participation in the United Nations, militarily through Allied occupation, and economically through the Marshall Plan and extended private networks of trade. Following the war, Americans acquired a new global awareness brought about by immigration, intermarriage, travel, and more formally through agencies such as the United Nations Food and Agricultural Organization (FAO), United Nations Educational,

Scientific, & Cultural Organization (UNESCO), and later the United States' own Agency for International Development (AID), the Peace Corps, and perhaps most importantly through the military that maintained a strong presence around the world. Banking, petroleum, agriculture, aircraft, and automobiles led in the vanguard of American overseas business expansion.

In the fifty years between 1945 and 1995, at least five major conditions contributed significantly to the development of a global economy and to the sense of a global community. The first was the explosion of the atomic bomb in August 1945. These effects continue to unfold. Perhaps one of its lasting impacts worldwide has been to cause humankind to think about both the vulnerability of life on Earth and the commonality of life. The atomic bomb, followed closely by the end of World War II, the prolonged Cold War, the entry into space by the Soviet Union and the United States and the continuing impact of space technology on the world, and finally the end of the Cold War lead the list of major influences on the development of the global economy.

Certainly the end of World War II set the stage for what would follow. The costs of war were enormous. An estimated 45 million people lost their lives. Nations, friend and foe, were devastated. The close of hostilities left many European economies in a state of collapse. Businesses and international trade structures, already undermined by the worldwide depression of the 1930s, had to be rebuilt. Most nations had enormous national debts, if their economies survived at all. Secretary of State George C. Marshall even thought that while "the physical loss of life, the visible destruction of cities, factories, mines, and railroads" constituted enormous devastation, the most critical problem was "the dislocation of the entire fabric of European economy."

Few nations, including the United States, produced adequate consumer products for their domestic markets, much less for world markets. Great Britain, once boasting the world's strongest economy, became almost wholly dependent upon outside food supplies. The prewar leader in manufacturing exports and reexports, Great Britain now had virtually no peacetime consumer products to offer in world trade that could generate vital income for imports. Italy, France, and Greece were beset with communist movements that fed upon the economic prostration and sought total political collapse. Germany, Poland, and much of the Soviet Union lay in ruins. Many Japanese cities had been destroyed. China was in the throes of civil war and lacked modern industrial manufactures, excluding those that survived in formerly Japanese-occupied Manchuria. Out of this dissolution and destruction emerged a remarkably stable, but divided world.

The United States provided the key to global postwar economic recovery and reconstruction. Largely unscathed by the war, the United States developed an enormous industrial capacity during the war. War materials production was valued at approximately $60 billion in 1943, three times the 1941 level, and constituted 31 percent of the Gross National Product (GNP) compared with 9 percent in 1941. Military-aircraft production in 1943 was twice that of 1941, and the 1943 production of warships doubled that of 1941. GNP expanded from about $100 billion in 1940 to $121 billion in 1945. The index of industrial production increased to 239 compared to the 1935–1939 average of 100. Farm production in World War II exceeded that of World War I by 50 percent. Per capita production rose 25 percent during the war. Personal income rose from the 1929 prewar high of $654 per individual to $1090. Personal savings rose to an all-time high, in large part because during the war consumer goods were scarce, and wartime rationing and price controls discouraged consumption. In addition, as Eliot Janeway described in *The Economics of Crisis: War, Politics and the Dollar,* during World War II much of the world's money took refuge in the United States. The end of the war left the United States in the role of the world's banker, with most of the world's money in the bank.

The close of the war also left the United States with the most powerful military forces in the world—a military power buttressed by having exclusive possession of the atomic bomb. President Harry S. Truman promised that despite demobilization, the United States would remain the greatest military power on earth. In Central Park in New York City on October 27, during "Navy Day" celebrations, Truman described the changing scene: "Now we are in the process of demobilizing our naval force. We are laying up ships. We are breaking up aircraft squadrons. We are rolling up bases and releasing officers and men." But when our demobilization is all finished as planned, he added, the United States will still have the greatest naval power on earth and one of the most powerful air forces; with universal military training (that he was asking Congress to adopt), the United States could mobilize a powerful and well-equipped land, sea, and air force. A standing army marked a radical departure in American history. Traditionally, following wars, America demobilized and returned full time to peace. The United States, with rare exceptions, clung to its isolationist preferences since the time of the American Revolution. Americans historically preferred the Jeffersonian image of the United States in the world as the "Isle of Liberty," a refuge to be seen and heard, but not to be touched. This changed following World War II.

Why would the United States assume this new global posture? It was not, Truman emphasized, in order that the United States might obtain "one inch of territory in any place in the world." Rather, "we seek to use our military strength solely to preserve the peace of the world." We must enforce the terms of peace imposed upon our defeated enemies and fulfill the military obligations required of our membership in the United Nations. The goal is a lasting peace, maintained by force, if necessary. American postwar planning drew heavily upon the cooperative mode of the Atlantic Charter, agreed to by Winston Churchill and Franklin D. Roosevelt during their first conference aboard the destroyer *U.S.S. Augusta* off Newfoundland in August 1941. The Atlantic Charter set these three Allied objectives of war: a renunciation of territorial aggrandizement, the right of free peoples to determine their own form of government, and free trade and international economic cooperation. These goals were incorporated in the Declaration of the United Nations approved in January 1942 by twenty-six nations including the Soviet Union and the United States. The Atlantic Charter and the United Nations, in turn, led to the establishment of international financial and economic institutions including the International Monetary Fund (IMF), the International Bank for Reconstruction and Development (the World Bank), and the General Agreement on Tariffs and Trade (GATT).

Delegates from forty-four member nations of the United Nations met at Bretton Woods, New Hampshire in 1944, during the height of World War II, to create an international monetary system that would facilitate postwar trade and prevent the trade wars and financial instability that followed World War I. The United States, Great Britain, and the Soviet Union were major organizers of the conference, but the Soviet Union later withdrew.

The conference approved an international monetary system based on adjustable or pegged exchange rates. Under what is termed the Bretton Woods System, national currencies did not float free, nor were they tied directly to gold as had been customary before. Rates were adjustable. Exchange rates were agreed to between countries for purposes of commercial and financial transactions. If those rates became imbalanced, a nation could restore the balance by devaluation or revaluation and set or peg a new exchange rate. A country could also adjust its currency values to another currency by as much as 10 percent without approval of the International Monetary Fund, which became the supervisory agency for international exchange. Although the par value of a currency was stated in gold, the value of gold was in fact tied to the American dollar—fixed at $35 per ounce. Thus, gold did provide a measure of currency values, but did not literally dictate those values. This dollar–gold system provided a remarkably stable exchange base that contributed significantly to the dispersion of trade throughout much of the world (or as it came to be the Western world) between 1945 and 1971. In 1968 the Bretton Woods System began to collapse and was abandoned in 1973, but it is credited by many with having been the critical element in postwar recovery and world economic expansion. The Bretton Woods conferees also established a World Bank designed to help finance reconstruction and recovery, and it established the processes for international agreements on tariffs and trade (GATT), thus preventing or discouraging the disastrous trade wars of earlier times.

With an estimated two-thirds of the world's gold supplies in the United States at the close of World War II, and with the capacity to produce fully one-half of the world's agricultural and industrial products, the economy of the United States was critical to postwar recovery. Indeed, economists and others debate the real significance of the Bretton Woods agreements. Some argued that when postwar prosperity came, it came as a product of market realities, rather than of the Bretton Woods Conference. That may be true to an extent. It is also likely that had there been no such agreements, the autonomous and diversified economies of the world would have reverted to the isolationist, protective policies of the past and thus locked out the "realities of the international marketplace." It is also true, as will be discussed in following chapters, that the centrality of the United States to the global economy and the character of the international marketplace has changed markedly in the past half-century. Bretton Woods, however, set the style and tone for international trade and commerce for almost a quarter-century. During that time the U.S. economy was dominant.

The exigencies of war thus created a new level of international economic cooperation that simply had not existed before. Whether that spirit of international cooperation and world economic integration would survive the peace following the war remained to be seen.

In 1945 President Truman identified twelve points or principles that he thought were recognized as fundamental to American foreign policy in the postwar world. Reminiscent of the Pan-American pledges of earlier times, Truman pledged cooperation with other American nations to preserve the territorial integrity and the political independence of the nations of the Western Hemisphere. But the twelve points went far beyond the hemispheric policies of the Monroe Doctrine. They reflected in part President Woodrow Wilson's Fourteen Points enunciated as guidelines for achieving a lasting peace after World War I. They also echoed the commitments of the Atlantic Charter and the United Nations. The United States had begun to think in global terms.

Truman defined the American position after World War II as affirming these beliefs: 1) no U.S. territorial expansion; 2) the return of sovereign rights and self-government to all peoples who have been deprived of them by force; 3) no territorial changes in any friendly part of the world unless they accord with the freely expressed wishes of the people concerned; 4) the right of all peoples to choose their own form of government without interference; 5) in cooperation with Allies, help for defeated enemy states to establish peaceful, democratic governments; and 6) refusal to recognize any government imposed upon any nation by the force of any foreign power. Truman reiterated basic economic beliefs that the United States had espoused since the time of its own revolution.

These beliefs included the ideas that 7) *all nations should have the freedom of the seas and equal rights to the navigation of boundary rivers and waterways, and rivers and waterways that pass through more than one country;* 8) *all states accepted in the society of nations should have access on equal terms to the trade and raw materials of the world;* 9) the states of the Western Hemisphere should work as good neighbors to solve their common problems; 10) *full economic collaboration between all nations, great and small, is essential to the improvement of living conditions all over the world and to the establishment of freedom from fear and freedom from want;* 11) the U.S. would continue to promote freedom of expression and freedom of religion throughout the peace-loving areas of the world; and finally, 12) the preservation of peace among nations required a United Nations organization willing jointly to use force if necessary to ensure peace.

Although Truman admitted that these objectives would not soon be achieved (and certainly were not achieved), nevertheless "it is our policy; and we shall seek to achieve it." It is in the latter context that Truman's guidelines for American foreign policy after the war are so important. For the most part, the United States did adhere in policy to the precepts. Irrespective of how fully the United States was able to achieve open seas and open markets, the policy did provide a benchmark or sense of order for the development of international relations and postwar trade. An understanding of the development of the global economy requires an understanding to the context in which that economy developed. American military power, the United Nations, NATO, and American principles of free trade were powerful stimulants to restructuring the postwar world. The most powerful stimulants were American money and American agricultural and industrial products. Truman and most economists realized that the crucial ingredient to world economic recovery would be the protection and strengthening of the domestic economy. However, in 1945 and 1946, the domestic economy faced an uncertain and chaotic future.

There were problems. Converting from war to peacetime production would be costly and time-consuming. Demobilization meant transferring almost five million men from the military to the domestic economy. By 1946, U.S. military forces released some 3.5 million men and women from active duty. Concurrently, civilian employment declined by 2.5 million. Many women who filled wartime manufacturing and service positions left the workforce. But Congress, fortuitously, provided a remarkable program for transferring military personnel to civilian life—and more significantly—a program that prepared those men and women for unusually productive lives in a rapidly changing world. The GI Bill of Rights provided returning veterans educational benefits to continue their education or to acquire new skills and loans for starting new businesses. But the long-range benefits extended far beyond demobilization. The long-term result was to provide the United States with the most educated and well-trained workforce of any nation in the world. It was a workforce peculiarly suited for the technical and scientific revolutions already afoot and for the development of international trade and commerce.

The present seemed beset with difficulties. Unemployment climbed rapidly after the close of hostilities; inflation even more. Many Americans, if not most, predicted a postwar depression as had followed World War I. Even though wages rose by 50 percent during the five years of war, prices rose only 30 percent because of wage and price controls. The lack of consumer goods such as automobiles, shoes, and civilian clothing, coupled with the flow of dollars from savings threatened severe price inflation. Price controls, established during the war but maintained after the war ended, became increasingly ineffective and unpopular through 1946. President Truman insisted on an extension of price controls after the expiration date of June 1946. When Congress passed a weakened price control law, Truman vetoed the bill. Congress passed an acceptable law in July, but in the thirty-day interim when no controls were in effect, the price index jumped by 10 percent.

Organized labor, now on the lagging end of the wage-price spiral and suffering layoffs and the loss of overtime, and chafing from the voluntary and involuntary wage controls of the war, erupted with a series of strikes beginning in 1946. The Brotherhood of Locomotive Engineers and Railway Trainmen called a general strike, halting rail traffic across the country for the first time in half a century. President Truman demanded an end to it and asked Congress for authority to draft the workers and court-martial them if they refused to return to work. A settlement was reached without this drastic action, but confrontations increased.

In November 1946, John L. Lewis, head of United Mine Workers, announced a strike in the bituminous-coal industry. Wartime price and production controls still applied, and the government, for all practical purposes, ran the mines. The Court issued an injunction prohibiting the strike. President Truman threatened to draft any who struck. The union struck anyway. Strikers were cited for contempt of court and ordered back to work. While the process unfolded, the government negotiated a settlement with the strikers, granting them most of their demands. Despite his strong antistrike sentiments, Truman was concerned about the plight of the laborer in America in the midst of demobilization and the pressures of inflation.

Laborers and farmers particularly suffered. Truman's domestic program had three major objectives: 1) control inflation; 2) assure a fair share of the national income to labor, business, and agriculture; and 3) provide a decent standard of living to every American. Truman consistently emphasized the interdependence of labor, business, agriculture, and *government* in sustaining postwar recovery and in promoting economic growth.

The Employment Act of 1946 effectively signaled the sustainment of the New Deal and the continuing role of government in the postwar domestic economy. Its provisions espoused "economic stabilization through government supplementation of private activity." The Act contained four major provisions. The first declared that it would be the continuing policy and responsibility of the federal government to coordinate and utilize all its plans, functions and resources with a view to creating and maintaining, in a manner calculated to foster and promote free competitive enterprise and the general welfare, conditions under which there will be afforded useful employment opportunities, including self-employment, for those able, willing and seeking to work, and to promote maximum employment, production and purchasing power.

In addition, the Act required the president to prepare an annual economic report "setting forth the current and projected levels of employment, production and purchasing power," and recommendations for actions needed to strengthen the economy. The Act authorized the creation of a three-person Council of Economic Advisers to "serve as an analytical and advisory unit to the President," and it established a joint Committee on the Economic Report to include seven members respectively from the House and the Senate. The Employment Act of 1946 not only placed the federal government in the role of caretaker for national economic welfare, but by inference and extrapolation it conferred upon that government a degree of responsibility for the encouragement of foreign trade and commerce, and conceivably for the welfare of peoples of other lands subjected to starvation, pestilence, and war. The encouragement of foreign trade, and at least the passive ideal that America offered hope for the hungry and dispossessed of the world, were not wholly new.

American isolationist policies, such as they were in the past, generally had been much more rhetorical and intellectual than economic. Laissez-faire meant not only "leave us alone," but also leave us free to engage in foreign trade and commerce wherever American business and ships find markets. When President Thomas Jefferson responded to a declaration of war by Tripoli with an attack on the Barbary pirates who levied tribute on American (and other) commerce, Jefferson was incongruously defending American principles of laissez-faire. It must be remembered that during the approximately 175 years of colonial dependency on Great Britain or other European powers, American colonies were intimately and intensely participating in international if not global trade and commerce. Despite the Revolution and the American preference for independence and isolation, American products, prominently cotton, tobacco, rice, ships, naval stores, fish, and beef found world markets throughout the nineteenth century. As American manufactured goods began to enter world markets in the 1880s and 1890s, the American government became more active in protecting American commerce. Thus, the major foreign policy of the United States at the turn of the twentieth century was to maintain an "open door" for American business throughout the world. Truman's advocacy of freedom of the seas and "access on equal terms to the trade and raw materials of the world" followed a well-established precedent of governmental participation in promoting trade and commerce. Finally, America long prided itself as being the land of opportunity for the poor and the oppressed, if those people could reach American shores.

However, the disruptions brought by the conversion from war to peace produced a host of divergent and often extreme attitudes and positions, particularly as related to the role of government in the economy and to the role of the United States in world affairs. Senator Robert A. Taft of Ohio pointed to the loss of the old individualism and personal freedom that government involvement threatened. Henry A. Wallace, Truman's secretary of agriculture, on the other extreme, accused Truman of selling out to "monopoly capitalism." Wallace wanted government to play a dominant role in restructuring the American economy. Meanwhile, the South, fearful of "big government" and the disruption of traditional segregation patterns, organized to defend "states rights." Obviously, these were difficult and painful years that threatened to tear the country apart rather than restore it. Strikes, shortages, and inflationary pressures continued throughout 1946 into 1947. As inflation lowered the value of employee paychecks, unions ordered strikes for higher pay. The public blamed the strikes for accelerating inflation.

Congress approved the Taft-Hartley Labor Management Relations bill in spring 1947. The bill sought to curb the "excesses" of the labor movement and impede the postwar wage-price spiral. The Taft-Hartley Act outlawed the "closed shop," by which unions required membership in the union as a condition for employment. The Act required formal notification of a strike at least sixty days prior to the termination of a labor contract. It also authorized the president to use the injunction against a strike that endangered national safety or health. The bill likewise prohibited unfair union practices such as secondary boycotts and the refusal to bargain in good faith. It required unions to register with the secretary of labor and submit annual financial reports to the secretary. President Truman, declaring the act a "shocking piece of legislation," issued a ringing veto. Congress overrode the veto and the bill became law.

Capitalism seemed to be on trial, at home and abroad. Truman identified inflation as the main culprit. The cost of home furnishings had risen 23 percent since 1945; clothing was 24 percent higher, and food 31 percent. Wholesale prices were advancing more rapidly than consumer prices. Farm products were up 40 percent, building materials 51 percent, and food 53 percent. For a time the United States was the major source of farm products for the world. There was, Truman said, a phenomenal world demand for American farm products, which, coupled with the unprecedented purchasing power of the American consumer, combined to force farm prices upward. It was not, he stressed in answer to critics, government farm price support programs that caused the price inflation. Price supports for wheat ($1.82 a bushel), and hogs ($14.94 per hundredweight), for example, were markedly below market prices of wheat at $2.50 per bushel and hogs at $25 per hundredweight. Truman advocated high taxes, credit controls, rent controls, and export controls as mechanisms for curbing inflation. But he also believed that "we are beginning to sense the fact . . . that our peace-time economy cannot only equal our war-time economy, but can surpass it."

He insisted that the assurance of American economic well-being could come only by providing assistance in the reconstruction and rehabilitation of countries devastated by war:

> And only if we maintain and increase our prosperity can we expect other countries to recognize the full merits of a free economy. We know that our system of private competitive enterprise has produced the highest standard of living the world has ever seen. By steadily raising this standard, we can demonstrate to all other nations the vitality and superiority of a free economy. Our system of private enterprise is now being tested before the world. If we can prove that it is more productive and more stable, more generous and more just than any other economic system, we shall have won the test.

American capitalism, thus, set itself not only to compete in world markets, but also to compete with fascism, socialism, and communism as a way of life. Within a few years the enormity of that competition began to emerge.

Following agreements made by Winston Churchill, Joseph Stalin, and Franklin D. Roosevelt at Yalta in February 1945, and subsequently at Potsdam between Truman, Churchill, and Stalin, the Allies agreed to the occupation of territories captured from the enemy by the troops respectively of Great Britain, the Soviet Union, France, and the United States. When the war ended, the Soviet Union took control of Poland, East Germany, Yugoslavia, and Bulgaria in Europe and Manchuria, Outer Mongolia, North Korea, the Kurile Islands, and

Sakhalin Island in the Far East. The Soviet Union also sought to exercise control over Greece and Turkey, which would open the Soviet Union to the Dardanelles and the Mediterranean—giving her the long cherished access to the Atlantic. Civil war between communists and nationalists erupted in Greece and was threatened in Turkey. By 1947 the United States had withdrawn most of its armies from Europe. Naval ships were being mothballed and the aircraft stacked in Southwest desert reserves.

Then Great Britain informed the Truman administration that it could no longer provide financial or economic aid to Greece or to Turkey, nor could it sustain its commitments in several parts of the world, including Greece:

> Greece is today without funds to finance the importation of those goods which are essential to bare subsistence. Under these circumstances the people of Greece cannot make progress in solving their problems of reconstruction. Greece is in desperate need of financial and economic assistance to enable it to resume purchases of food, clothing, fuel, and seeds. These are indispensable for the subsistence of its people and are obtainable only from abroad. Greece must have help to import the goods necessary to restore internal order and security so essential for economic and political recovery.

The government of Greece made an urgent appeal to the United States for assistance. American assistance is imperative, Truman told Congress, if Greece is to survive as a free nation. Meanwhile, Turkey also asked for assistance to "effect the modernization necessary for the maintenance of its national integrity." Following the requests, Truman asked Congress to appropriate $400 million for financial and economic assistance to Greece and Turkey as "an investment in world freedom and world peace." The Truman Doctrine, as the policy came to be called, committed the United States "to support free peoples who are resisting attempted subjugation by armed minorities or by outside pressures." It marked the first independent step by the United States outside the structures of the United Nations to become the self-anointed protector of the Western world and provided the first formal mechanism for the independent dispersion of American financial assistance abroad.

The rising American concern for global justice and the defense of democratic institutions also contributed to important reforms on the domestic front. The worldwide reaction against Nazi ethnic persecutions and the plight of dispossessed and minority groups throughout the world initiated a reawakening of Americans to the plight of minority groups within their own country. President Truman again took the initiative by asking Congress for legislation to remedy a broad range of social problems. He proposed the creation of a permanent commission on civil rights and the strengthening of existing civil rights statutes, federal assurance for voting rights, federal protection against lynching, the creation of a fair employment practice commission, and a prohibition of discrimination in interstate transportation. He sought legislation to provide home rule for the District of Columbia, statehood for Alaska and Hawaii, more opportunity for residents to become naturalized citizens, and for settlement of claims by Japanese Americans resulting from their wartime relocation and internment. The product was slow and incremental, but there were, over time, significant improvements. In time, more Americans did acquire equal opportunities for jobs, homes, health, and education. Concurrently, the United States obtained a more productive and trained workforce.

Not only population growth but also the changing characteristics of the workforce provided a measure of direction for the growth of the American economy following World War II. Quota laws, combined with depression and war, had reduced the flow of immigrants to the United States. With a population of approximately 144 million in 1945, the United States was culturally a more homogeneous place than it had ever been. It also stood on the brink of a veritable population explosion as a result of the decline in the formation of families and new births during the years of war and depression.

Population growth and migration have been critical elements affecting post–World War II relationships. World populations more than doubled in the fifty years following World War II, from approximately 2 billion in 1945 to 5.6 billion in 1995. During the previous one hundred years (1850–1950) world populations doubled from roughly one to two billion people. World populations are expected to double again during the next one hundred years (which would occur assuming a considerably slower rate of growth than in the past half-century). Population growth and greater competition for scarce resources in turn stimulated new waves of migration. More than one million people migrate into the United States each year. Since 1945 about one-half of the new immigrants have come from Latin America, one-fourth from Europe, and one-fourth from Asia. The population of the United States almost doubled in the same fifty-year period from about 135 million to 260 million. The median age actually declined during the postwar baby boom, but has risen overall from about thirty in 1945 to thirty-three in 1995. One hundred and fifty years earlier, the median age was almost half (eighteen) what it is today. Postwar America is characterized by the formation of new households and an aging and more affluent population. Population growth and migration were vital stimulants to domestic expansion and increasing world trade.

Indeed, by the close of 1947 the United States stood on the threshold of what were, in retrospect, ten amazing years. *U.S. News and World Report* concluded in a December 1957 article that the past ten years were "a time of change and accomplishment unmatched in the history of America." Americans had become the world's most prosperous people. And there were 28 million more of them than in 1947. In 1947, television was still an idea more than a reality; commercial aircraft were converting from two engines to four; superhighways were still something peculiar to Germany; supermarkets and the suburbs were yet to come; automobiles lacked automatic transmissions, power brakes, and tubeless tires; most homes and commercial buildings were not air-conditioned; antibiotics and polio vaccines did not exist. Over the next decade many, if not most Americans came to have and enjoy these innovations, as well as automatic dishwashers, garbage disposals, FM radios, interstate highways, and miracle drugs. By the close of the decade, jet aircraft were replacing the four-engine piston-driven aircraft on commercial passenger flights.

Thirty-nine million babies were born in the United States in the decade between 1947 and 1957. Eleven million new homes were built. Twenty-five million new cars were sold. Almost every home had a television set by 1957, and Americans moved from the city to the suburbs. More Americans completed high school, and far more completed college than ever before. Personal earnings totaled 2.6 trillion dollars. Americans saved $160 billion. Americans spent $33 billion for new schools, hospitals, and government buildings, $28 billion for new highways, $55 billion for offices, factories, and stores, $40 billion on public utilities, and $110 billion for new houses and apartments. During the decade, the United States spent $300 billion for defense, and gave $50 billion in foreign aid and assistance.

By the close of the decade, despite the dramatic growth, the Cold War, rather than peace and prosperity, had come to dominate the thoughts and actions of the United States and many of the nations of the world. Even though the end of World War II, and indeed the war itself, generated a new level of interaction and collaboration among nations, the Cold War intensified the competition for markets, resources, and technology, and perhaps incongruously led to yet additional remarkable decades of change.

Sputnik, launched on October 4, 1957, also changed the world and our perceptions of that world. "I was at my ranch in Texas," Lyndon Baines Johnson recalled, "when news of Sputnik flashed across the globe . . . and simultaneously a new era of history dawned over the world." While Sputnik and the American response to Sputnik quickly became entangled in the nuances of Cold War competition, the human entry into space signaled by the flight of Major Yury Gagarin on April 12, 1961, and Alan Shepard on May 5, 1961, changed the world as we thought it to be. The lunar landing on July 18, 1969, confirmed the change. Humankind was not Earthbound. That realization had an impact similar to the discovery by Copernicus that the Earth revolved about the sun, rather than that the Earth was the center of the universe (as we thought for thousands of years). Things we thought could not be—were. Things we formerly could not think—were thought.

Ordinary market demands, coupled with the Cold War, intensified American involvement in the world after 1945. Indeed, had it not been for the competition with and fear of the Soviet Union, the United States very likely would have returned home after World War II to resume its traditional and respected distance—if not isolation—from the outside world. But the Cold War changed that: The Cold War accelerated the rate of technological innovation and change. It led the United States to perpetuate and build the North Atlantic Treaty Organization (NATO) and the Southeast Asia Treaty Organization (SEATO). It made every nation and every people a point of concern and competition. The world became divided between East and West, communist and democratic, "theirs" and "ours." The world ceased being an anomalous cluster of hundreds of nations and peoples and for a time became more or less two clusters of nations and peoples. And each people, each nation, no matter how remote, became a point of interest and contention between the two centers of world power. The Cold War forced a new era of integration within the Soviet bloc and within the West. It also brought about the Marshall Plan. The Marshall Plan proved singularly responsible for the economic character of the postwar world.

Chapter 2

THE MARSHALL PLAN

The Marshall Plan had more to do with defining the character of the postwar global economy than any other single event or factor. A product or consensus of the perceptions of many American leaders, including President Harry S. Truman and George F. Kennan, the American ambassador to the Soviet Union, and Dwight D. Eisenhower, commander in chief of Allied Forces, and George C. Marshall, secretary of state, the Marshall Plan provided the channel for the reconstruction of Europe and for the creation of a bilateral economic union in which the United States maintained hegemony or dominance for almost twenty-five years.

Indeed, the developing global economy has had three distinct phases. The first is that characterized by Eastern and Western economic unions from approximately 1948 to 1973. In the East, the Soviet Union and communism exercised dominance. In the West, the Marshall Plan and American capitalism set the tone. During the second phase, stretching from approximately 1973 to 1989, the Western economic union experienced realignment. European Economic Cooperation (EEC) gave way to European Union (EU). Japan became a major economic power in the Pacific, its influence extending through Southeast Asia on the one hand, and west to United States, Canada, and South America. While strong, the United States no longer dominated economic affairs in the West. The European Union, the United States, and Japan and Southeast Asia shared power. A form of Western economic federalism developed. The third phase of the global economy began in 1989 with the dissolution of the Soviet-Communist block and the development of a new pluralistic and essentially capitalistic world order where economic power was shared through economic and trading coalitions centered about the European Union, the United States, Japan and Southeast Asia, and Russia. China became a fifth center of influence in the global market economy. Each coalition interacts (and competes) with the other to form something of a global confederation of trading coalitions. It is a global community still loosely and somewhat uncertainly constructed on a capitalist persuasion, peaceful coexistence, and creative cooperation and is very much in the formative stages.

The inception of the integrated global economy had much to do with the Marshall Plan. Approved by the United States Congress in 1948, the Marshall Plan was a catalyst in the construction of a new global economic order. It provided immediate relief and initiated the reconstruction of war-torn Europe, and it established a new element of economic interdependence among nations. Many believed, as did President Truman, that European recovery was essential to the welfare of the American economy. "The last two decades have taught us the bitter lesson that no economy, not even one so strong as our own, can remain healthy and prosperous in a world of poverty and want," Truman explained when he called upon Congress to approve a program for sustained U.S. aid to Europe. The president added:

> In the past, the flow of raw materials and manufactured products between Western Europe, Latin America, Canada and the United States has integrated these areas in a great trading system. In the same manner, Far Eastern exports to the United States have helped pay for the goods shipped from Europe to the Far East. Europe is thus an essential part of a world trading network. The failure to revive fully this vast trading system, which has begun to function again since the end of the war, would result in economic deterioration throughout the world. The United States, in common with other nations, would suffer.

Truman explained that the initial problem following the end of the war had been to prevent widespread starvation and disease. That had been largely accomplished, but real economic recovery was faltering. A particularly bitter winter, floods, and then drought cut European grain crops to historic lows and compounded the difficulties. The problem, Truman said, was essentially a European problem.

Even with outside aid Europe could not accomplish the goals of recovery unless European nations reached common goals and a cooperative plan.

Now Truman said they had done so, in part at the instigation of the United States. On June 5, 1947, Secretary of State George Marshall advised European nations that further assistance from the United States would follow only if Europe agreed upon its basic needs and agreed to take cooperative steps to accomplish a comprehensive plan of recovery. In July, representatives of sixteen European nations met in Paris and formed a Committee of European Economic Cooperation (CEEC). The countries represented included Austria, Belgium, Denmark, France, Greece, Iceland, Ireland, Italy, Luxembourg, the Netherlands, Norway, Portugal, Sweden, Switzerland, Turkey, and the United Kingdom. West Germany, still occupied by the Allied forces, was not formally represented at the meeting. The CEEC sent a report on its conditions and needs to the United States in September.

That report characterized the economy of Europe as a trading community that historically depended upon international trade for survival. Some 270 million people, occupying a relatively small area, enjoyed a relatively high standard of living by manufacturing imported raw materials and exporting the finished products to the world. Its farmland was basically insufficient to sustain its populations. Europe was dependent upon imports for its food and fuels. In the past Europe paid for its imports by exporting. But the disruptions and devastation of war had destroyed factories, equipment, and capital. Europe could not manufacture and export, nor buy the raw materials, fuel, food, and fiber from abroad. The Committee of European Economic Cooperation reported that "shortages of raw materials, productive capacity, and exportable commodities have set up vicious circles of increasing scarcities and lowered standards of living."

That circle, Truman said, must be broken by enabling Europe to increase production to the point that it could import sufficient goods for its survival and welfare. The European Economic Community (EEC) had agreed to banking and financial cooperation (that is, the European Payments Union, which led in 1958 to the creation of the European Monetary Agreement), the reduction of trade barriers, and the removal of obstacles to the free movement of persons within Europe. In effect, the previously fiercely independent and sovereign European nations agreed that Europe should take initial steps in de-

President Truman signs the $6,098,000 global aid bill to help economic recovery abroad and combat communism. Pictured left to right: Arthur Vandenberg, John Snyder, Charles Eaton, Tom Connally, Julius Krug, Joe Martin, Sol Bloom, and Clinton P. Anderson.

(UP/Bettmann Newsphotos)

veloping itself as a "common market." What Europe needed now were large quantities of food, fuel, raw materials, and capital equipment. The only country with sufficient economic strength that could provide the financial aid to remedy the "temporary gap between minimum European needs and war-diminished European resources" was the United States.

On December 19, 1947, Truman asked Congress for an initial appropriation of $6.8 billion for the first fifteen months of an estimated four-year assistance program to provide aid to European countries in obtaining imports essential to genuine economic recovery that they could not finance from their own resources. The administration estimated that an additional appropriation of $10.2 billion would be needed so that by 1952 Europe might become economically stable and self-sufficient.

The European Economic Recovery Plan (Marshall Plan) provided money in the form of outright grants and loans. Repayment of loans would be conditioned by the ability of the nation to pay. Nations that borrowed or received grants would not be required to spend the money in the United States. As time passed, it was anticipated that loans from the International Bank, and private banks, would comprise an increasing portion of assistance to Europe. Truman cited studies by the secretary of interior gauging the impact of foreign purchases on American raw material supplies and markets, one by the Council of Economic Advisers attesting to the capacity of the economy to absorb the assistance and the new production required to meet European demands and a study by the secretary of commerce with businessmen concluding that financial assistance would be proper, wise, and necessary.

The Marshall Plan had many sources. George Marshall was one. Marshall announced the general outline of the proposed program designed to restore confidence of the people of Europe in their own economic future in June 1947. President Truman consistently stressed the need to provide world stability by attacking hunger and starvation. George F. Kennan, ambassador to the Soviet Union, may have instigated the Marshall Plan when he published an anonymous article in the July 1947 issue of *Foreign Affairs,* advising containment of the Soviet system. Dwight D. Eisenhower, military governor of U.S.-occupied West Germany who replaced Marshall as Army chief of staff, seemed predisposed to a plan of economic assistance for Europe. He commented in his diaries on May 15, 1947, that "there are so many nations needing our help that the whole job seems appalling," but to help them would be to help ourselves. Great Britain, France, Italy, Greece, and Turkey most needed assistance, but Eisenhower thought that West Germany and Austria would soon need assistance:

> I believe the best thing we could now do would be to post 5 billion to the credit of the secretary of state and tell him to use it to support democratic movements wherever our vital interests indicate. Money should be used to promote possibilities of self-sustaining economies, not merely to prevent immediate starvation.

In September, Eisenhower wrote that "the sullen weight of Russia" leans against capitalism, democracy, and independent nations. "Russia is definitely out to communize the world."

Despite the warnings of Henry A. Wallace and others on the one hand who believed that the United States could comfortably coexist with the Soviet Union, and the traditional isolationists on the other who would have no part of American involvement in overseas missions of whatever kind, Congress approved the Marshall Plan, and the American public gave it overwhelming support.

The Soviet Union proved distinctively less than enthusiastic. An intended recipient of Marshall Plan aid, the Soviet Union declined to accept economic assistance that required supervision of the Committee on European Economic Cooperation (later the Organization for European Cooperation). The Soviet Union became more concerned as the European alliance for economic cooperation strengthened under new agreements entered into at Luxembourg in March 1948. Moreover, the Western Allies abandoned their earlier intentions to maintain an economically weakened West Germany, but rather began plans to create a financially and industrially strong West German Republic with a large degree of autonomy, and with financial support under the Marshall Plan to aid in its economic recovery. Soviet concerns turned to distress.

In June 1948, the Soviet Union closed Berlin, a city administratively divided among the Big Four (the United States, Great Britain, France, and the Soviet Union) to the Western Allies. The West's choice at this point seemed either to send tanks into Berlin and begin a third world war or to abandon Berlin to the Soviet Union as the West had abandoned much of Eastern Europe to (as it turned out) permanent occupation by Soviet forces. The West did neither, even though the Soviet Union seized control of Czechoslovakia, brushing off efforts by Czechs to establish their independence from the Soviet Bloc. Rather, the Allies, led by the United States, initiated an airlift of vital cargoes to the beleaguered citizens of West Berlin. Now the initiative fell to the Soviet Union either to shoot down the Allied planes and begin a third world war or to do nothing and hope the West abandoned its airlift. The Soviet Union elected the latter. The Cold War had begun in earnest.

In the short term, the Cold War seemed to stem the rising course of globalism and served to divide the incipient global community into two hemispheres of influence. Yet, in another context, the ultimate construction of a global economy may have been assisted by a strengthening in the cooperation and integration of the Western economies. Although the Soviet Bloc also was economically integrated, that integration, unlike in the West, was by no means reciprocal. The communist system stymied capital investment, the growth of institutions of private property, free markets, and the overall economic development of the members of the Union of Soviet

Socialist Republics. Indeed, the Soviet Union steadfastly dismembered and undermined the productive capacity of East Germany and Poland in particular and most of the other Soviet satellites in general.

In contrast, the Marshall Plan, coupled with military spending and expansion and United Nations–sanctioned programs such as the United Nations Relief and Rehabilitation Administration (UNRRA) (which spent $1 billion for food, clothing, and supplies in the first three years after World War II) or the UN's Food and Agricultural Organization (FAO) (which provided for food production and distribution throughout the world), stimulated remarkably rapid recovery. Indeed, economic stimulation went far beyond mere recovery, so that within a decade the productive capacity of Europe and the West greatly exceeded that which had existed at the beginning of World War II—and that product continued to expand with relatively little interruption. The world has rarely, if ever, experienced the extent of economic expansion in so little time as occurred in the few decades following World War II. By the 1970s, European economic power had become competitive with American interests, forcing a reevaluation of the American role in the world economic order.

More immediately, the West responded to the initial Soviet threat in Europe by organizing the North Atlantic Treaty Organization (NATO), placing an allied army under a single command. Shortly after the organization of NATO, the Soviet Union revealed that it had produced an atomic bomb. The West responded by strengthening its NATO armaments and defenses. The United States halted demobilization and began a new peacetime mobilization. China collapsed to a communist takeover by Mao Tse-tung. The U.S.'s wartime ally, Chiang Kai-shek, fled with his nationalist armies to Formosa. In 1950, communist forces of North Korea (divided along the 38th parallel for Soviet and U.S. administration after World War II) attacked the Republic of South Korea. Supported by sanctions of the UN Security Council, President Truman sent American forces to the defense of South Korea. Just as American armies led by General Douglas MacArthur seemed close to occupying all of North Korea and ending the war, China threw thirty-three divisions across the Yalu River marking the Chinese–North Korean boundary and drove American forces back across the 38th parallel. Finally, in 1953, an armistice resulted in an armed and watchful peace along the 38th parallel. Between 1950 and 1953 American expenditures for defense rose from $13.2 to $50 billion and averaged about $43 billion for the remainder of

TABLE 2–1
U.S. Defense Expenditures as a Percentage of Total, 1940–1960

DEFENSE EXPENDITURES AS A PROPORTION OF TOTAL FEDERAL
EXPENDITURES, 1940–1960 (BILLIONS OF DOLLARS, CURRENT
PRICES).

Year	Defense Expenditures	Total Federal Expenditures	Defense Expenditures as a Percentage of Total Expenditures
1940	$ 1.8	$ 9.0	20.0
1941	6.2	13.0	46.6
1942	22.9	34.0	67.4
1943	63.3	79.4	79.7
1944	75.9	95.0	79.9
1945	80.5	98.3	81.9
1946	43.2	60.3	71.6
1947	14.8	38.9	38.0
1948	12.0	33.0	36.4
1949	14.0	39.5	35.4
1950	13.4	39.5	33.9
1051	20.9	44.0	47.5
1952	40.6	65.3	62.2
1953	44.1	74.1	59.5
1954	40.6	70.9	57.2
1955	35.6	68.5	52.0
1956	35.7	70.5	50.6
1957	38.7	76.5	50.6
1958	39.9	82.6	48.3
1959	44.6	92.1	48.4
1960	44.0	92.2	47.7

SOURCE: Historical Statistics of the United States Colonial Times to 1970, *Series Y 457-65, 1114.*

the decade. By 1968 defense expenditures exceeded $80 billion annually.

The Cold War resulted in the establishment of a permanent U.S. defense industry and more aggressive spending of American dollars in Europe and around the world. That in turn contributed to and hastened the creation of a new global civilization constructed upon science, technology, and, for a time at least, on war and the prospects of war. The arms race, which by the 1960s began to turn into a space race, greatly accelerated the pace of technological development throughout the world. Public spending, much of it funded by the United States as either Marshall Plan or defense spending, provided much of the market and incentive for expansion in the agricultural and manufacturing industries through the decades of the 1950s and 1960s and beyond.

Congress appropriated a total of $15.7 billion under Marshall Plan programs between 1949 and 1953 and another $7.7 billion in military aid under the Truman Doctrine. By 1960 U.S. foreign aid programs totaled almost $73 billion. As time passed, an increasingly larger portion of expenditures went to armaments. Whereas the United States spent about 15 percent of its budget on defense in 1940, in 1945 defense expenditures were 85 percent of the total budget, and while expenditures dropped precipitously to 35 percent in 1947, by 1952 defense expenditures again accounted for well more than one-half of federal expenditures. The following table illustrates defense expenditures as a percent of the total budget for the two decades from 1940 to 1960.

There is, of course, no certain correlation between U.S. defense expenditures and foreign aid disbursements and growth in the world's domestic product. There is no question that those nations benefited by U.S. assistance; those most closely associated with the United States in postwar trade and military liaisons were generally those that progressed most rapidly. The world's gross national product (GNP, in current dollars) rose from $0.7 trillion in 1950 to $3.2 trillion in 1970. U.S. GNP increased from $285 to $977 billion in the same two decades. The United States accounted for almost 40 percent of the world's GNP in 1950 and 30 percent in 1970, whereas the Soviet-Chinese systems remained remarkably stable at 23 to 25 percent of the world's total. European growth was pronounced, and Japanese growth phenomenal.

JAPAN: AN ECONOMIC REVOLUTION

Japan did more than recover from World War II. It effected what has become a remarkable economic revolution. That accomplishment does not stem from a Marshall Plan, but rather from a "MacArthur"

TABLE 2–2
World GNP

	1950	1960	1970
	100%	100%	100%
United States	39.3%	33.9%	30.2%
European Community	11.1%	12.7%	14.8%
United Kingdom	5.0%	4.8%	3.6%
Japan	1.5%	2.9%	6.2%
Other Developed	10.5%	10.9%	9.7%
Less Developed	9.1%	9.5%	10.0%
Communist USSR	13.5%	15.5%	16.6%
China	4.0%	4.5%	5.0%
Other	6.0%	5.3%	5.0%
Trillion US $ (current prices)	$0.7	$1.5	$3.2

plan, and, according to a 1968 study of the Constitution of Japan by Dan Fenno Henderson, from the "constructive and integrative response of the Japanese people themselves who have undertaken one of the broadest and to date most successful tasks of social engineering that the twentieth century has witnessed." Fundamental to that reconstruction and economic revolution has been the Japanese Constitution, drafted in the offices of the Supreme Commander for the Allied Powers (SCAP) General Douglas MacArthur, adopted by the Japanese Diet in 1947.

The Constitution met the prerequisites of the occupying powers, and most significantly, the specifications of the American government and the American people who wanted to abolish authoritarianism

TABLE 2–3
Index of Real GNP Growth

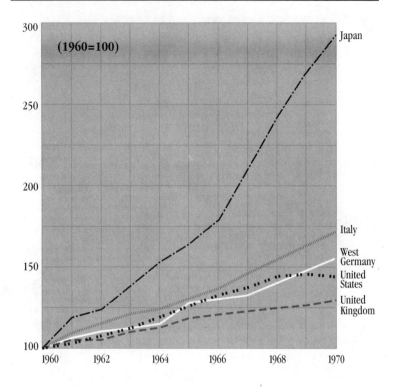

and militarism in Japan and to discourage—if not prevent—Japan from waging future wars of aggression. This aim conceivably could have been accomplished by dismantling the industrial resources of the country and exacting punitive damages as had been imposed on the Central Powers after World War I. That it was not attempted may in part be attributed to the failure of such policies at the close of that first great war.

In the adoption of their Constitution the Japanese people "forever renounce[d] war as a sovereign right of the nation and the threat or use of force as means of settling international disputes" and agreed not to maintain a standing army. The Constitution established sovereignty in the Japanese people—and no longer in the absolute sovereignty of the emperor and the preeminence of the state. Although the emperor remained as a "symbol of the State and of the

TABLE 2–4
Industrial Production Index

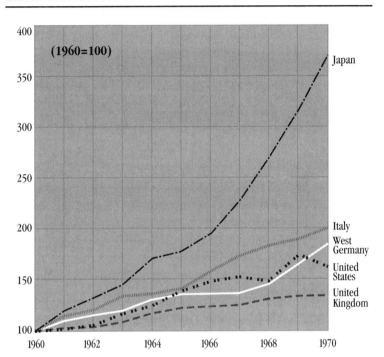

unity of the people," he derived his position from the will of the people. Paradoxically and remarkably, the Constitution seemed to coincide with a desire of the Japanese people to extirpate authoritarianism and militarism from their society and to broaden the base of individual economic opportunity. Individualism had long been submerged in prewar feudalistic/militaristic Japan.

That rejection of authoritarianism and militarism, according to studies by John M. Maki, a participant in a symposium sponsored by the Asian Law Program of the School of Law of the University of Washington twenty years after the adoption of the Constitution, derived from the fact that the Japanese people had experienced

> hundreds of thousands of military and civilian casualties at home and abroad; the disruption of patterns of family life by mobilization, the evacuation of cities, and the shifting of workers; the

destruction of family property and family resources directly and indirectly by military action; the destruction or draining away of untold national treasure; the destruction of cities and industrial installations of all kinds; near-starvation, malnutrition, illness and disease born of war and its consequences; the collapse of the dream of empire; the complete discrediting of both military and civilian leadership; the destruction of the old concept of the national destiny; and the collapse of a system of government and politics deemed not only superior but permanent.

And there were, in addition, similarities, relevances, and precedents in the new Constitution with the Meiji Constitution of 1889 and with the existing traditions, legal codes, and legal system to make the new Constitution acceptable and workable. To be sure, Japan by no means wholly rejected its past, and most certainly not the traditions that shape Japanese life and mores, but the Constitution did signal significant change in a society that tended to abhor change.

The Constitution contained relatively little about rights in property, except for the explicit protection contained in Article 29 that the "right to own or to hold property is inviolable." But that property might be taken by the state for public use with just compensation. Japanese legislation and the courts, however (drawing heavily upon the advice and expertise of the Supreme Commander of Allied Powers' Economic and Scientific Section and the Natural Resources Section), effected great reforms in land ownership, labor, and banking and finance. The result was to establish, in conjunction with the new political democracy, a broad-based economic democracy that facilitated individual pursuit of profit and property without undermining the collective welfare represented by the state and Japanese tradition.

The new laws effected a deconcentration of economic power from the traditional zaibatsu or large family combines that had controlled Japan's prewar economy, and they revoked the feudalistic tenant farm system that had effectively denied most Japanese farmers rights in property. More than half of Japan's labor force before World War II was engaged in agriculture and most of those as tenant farmers who paid absentee landlords 50 to 70 percent of the value of the crop in cash or kind. Industrial laborers, locked into limited and controlled labor markets, fared no better, if as well.

Labor laws, much in the spirit of the U.S. Employment Act of 1946, guaranteed fair and equitable wages to laborers. Land reforms, many of those effected through court action and by "peripheral" legislation, such as that creating farmer-controlled agricultural cooperatives, and government-funded agricultural experiment stations (both again in the tradition of the American cooperative agricultural programs) preserved the collectivist tradition of the Japanese feudal overlord, while guaranteeing to the family a fair (or as it turned out a remarkably comfortable) return on labor and capital.

The land reforms and farm legislation complemented Japan's interest in increasing rice production to compensate for the loss of its "rice basket" colonies (Korea and Taiwan) and in maintaining a secure domestic food supply. Rice production rose from 2.78 million hectares in 1946 to 3.31 million by 1960, and yields increased more than proportionately because of the introduction of scientific agriculture and improved technologies. Over time, price support programs and a "closed" market created large stocks of rice in government warehouses, very high price support/purchase expenditures, and a comfortable income and lifestyle for most Japanese farmers. The rice program became an item of considerable government expense and eventually contributed to external trade tensions—prominently with the United States.

Many factors other than the Constitution explain the Japanese economic "miracle," which raised the Japanese economy to the third most productive in the world. The interdependence of the Japanese economy with that of the United States initiated by military occupation was a determining element. The effectual release of the energies of the Japanese people achieved by political and economic reform contributed significantly.

Japanese output grew rapidly compared to that of the United States. From 1960 to 1973 the economic growth rate in Japan averaged 10 or 11 percent per year. Most of that increase is attributed to higher capital input and an increase in the level of Japanese technology. France and West Germany grew at a rate of 5.9 and 5.4 percent respectively, Italy at 4.8 percent, and the United Kingdom at 3.8. The U.S. rate of growth was a healthy 4.3 percent, considering that throughout the postwar period the U.S. economy maintained its position as the world's largest and the leader in output per capita.

As indicated in Table 2-1 (on page 25) although the U.S. share of world GNP declined from almost 40 percent in 1950 to 30 percent in 1970 (while Japan's rose from 1.5 to 6 percent and Europe's from 11 to 15 percent), in real terms the U.S. output grew in those two decades from about $300 million to more than $1 trillion, and the world's GNP increased almost fivefold. Through 1973 the United

States was the single largest importer of goods from Japan and Europe. Compared to Europe, Japan received relatively little financial aid and considerably less American capital, but the United States for a time was virtually the sole international market for Japanese manufactures and as late as 1990 consumed almost one-third of total Japanese exports. Japan became something of an economic adjunct to the American economy. Although basically symbiotic, the relationship also involved competition and conflict.

The overriding strength of the American economy, American assistance through programs such as the Marshall Plan, American capital investment, and the American marketplace that seemingly could not be satiated were primary incentives to both European and Japanese postwar recovery and economic expansion. The trade relationship fostered between the United States and Western Europe was reinforced by the Cold War.

The Cold War served to integrate the Western and Pacific Rim economies with most of those of the American hemisphere in a way impossible under purely voluntary or normal circumstances. The Cold War enforced a degree of hemispheric solidarity and integration despite underlying and traditional currents of national autonomy and economic independence, isolation, and self-sufficiency. But it also sublimated what may have been stronger and more overt manifestations of true and unfettered global trade and commerce on the other hand.

THE EMERGING STRUCTURE OF THE GLOBAL ECONOMY

Global trade and commerce, in the view of the United States and most of its Western allies and trading partners, required free trade and a nonrestrictive international financial system. The interpretation of what constituted free trade and an accessible international exchange system varied among the trading associates. The United States also believed that capitalism was much preferred to socialistic systems and that private property rights must be assured at home and abroad. Most U.S. allies and trading partners in Europe and in the Americas tended to be less supportive of free trade, capitalism, and rights in private property. The communist systems generally opposed all three.

Beneath these broad, essentially ideological persuasions, most nations in the West sought international trade and financial opportunities. The facilitation and expansion of that trade and commerce, in turn, led to the creation of various stages and types of economic union and degrees of economic integration. A basic phase of economic integration was the creation of a *free trade area,* in which member nations eliminate tariffs and quotas among themselves. As so often happens, these free trade associations, as was true in the case of the European Economic Community, did not eliminate all tariffs and quotas or they eliminated selected schedules only over a long period of time. Quite often, "free trade" may refer only to selected industries or products. Thus, one of the first and most effective free trade agreements entered into by European nations was the European Coal and Steel Community, which, beginning in 1952, generally provided free access and trade in the essential iron/coal/steel industries of Europe across national boundaries. Members of a free trade area preserve their essential economic autonomy and independence.

A *customs union* adds an important dimension to a free trade area by having all member states agree to a common tariff policy. Thus, the European Coal and Steel Commmunity rapidly evolved into the European Economic Community (EEC), formed by two Treaties of Rome in 1957. Members included France, West Germany, Belgium, Italy, the Netherlands, and Luxembourg. They agreed to pursue common tariff levels on imported steel, automobiles, farm products, wine, or other goods and to abolish or reduce tariffs between the member nations. Some items, particularly agricultural commodities, were for a time excluded from the customs union tariff schedules, but would be managed as the individual nation might prefer. Great Britain led in the organization in 1960 of a rival trading bloc, styled the European Free Trade Union (EFTA). Members included the United Kingdom, Sweden, Switzerland, Austria, Norway, Denmark, and Portugal. Later, in 1973, following several applications by Great Britain that France vetoed, the United Kingdom was admitted to the EEC, and other members of the EFTA either joined later or collaborated under a Special Relations Agreement.

The next stage following a customs union is the development of a common market or economic community. In a common market, not only are goods free to move within the union, but labor and capital are also free to move from one state to another. The laws, courts, and currency of the host state are still applicable, but there are no penalties or constraints on the employment of individuals from member nations or the investment of capital by parties from a member nation. To a considerable extent, a common market enjoys economic benefits similar to a federal union such as the United States, but it lacks a common currency and the overriding authority of uniform and enforceable federal laws relating to trade, commerce, and property rights. In addition, a common market does not have a central tax authority. It cannot build roads, bridges, or internal improvements beneficial to the common good. That, in turn, provides limits or constraints on commerce. The absence of a central authority partly can be overcome by unilateral agreements and treaties.

In comparing the United States to the European Economic Community, it should be emphasized that since its founding the United States comprised the largest free trade zone in the world. It uniquely enjoyed one set of laws, one currency, one postal system, a uniform code of navigation, an overriding and common tax policy set by federal authority, and the power and incentive to promote internal improvements. Internal improvements have historically included roads, canals, railroads, navigational improvements, and more recently air traffic facilities and controls. Common markets and the incipient global economy have not and are not likely to approach the model provided by the U.S. economy—and perhaps should not attempt to approach that model.

An *economic union,* such as that developing in Europe, removes some of the disabilities or encumbrances involved in the movement of goods and capital in a common market. Thus, the European Union (EU) concedes at least a degree of economic sovereignty to a central authority. The European Union is moving toward a common currency, a central bank, and a defined level or authority for supranational taxation. In theory an economic union provides a larger and less encumbered market with more opportunities for economies of scale and specialization with corresponding savings. The transaction costs of organizing an economy are lowered. A good part of transaction costs are government, banks, communications and transportation systems, legal systems, language differences, bureaucracies, competitive (or conflicting) currencies and tariffs, educational and informational systems, and the costs of developing new technology.

Generally, then, the stages of international economic integration are 1) the establishment of a free trade association, 2) the organization of a customs union, 3) the development of an economic community, and 4) the creation of an economic union. These modern stages, however, have largely been regional and hemispheric. They are highly conditioned by geography—and tend to involve contiguous national borders. Historically, the integrated units had cultural, language, and sometimes familial (aristocratic, royalty) affiliations and often were more truly international in scope than the current economic associations. We knew them then as colonial empires.

Whatever their character, these modern emerging economic associations among nations provide what would seem to be a necessary precursor to the creation of global economic associations. A global economic union is also conditioned by geography, but in the modern era geography has been tempered if not wholly altered by technology—including rapid communications and transportation systems. For example, the U.S. National Aeronautics and Space Administration (NASA) is largely responsible for the development of real-time worldwide communications and that in turn has created integrated global markets and reduced the costs of global trade.

The global economy will likely experience stages of development similar to those identified with regional economic integration. An incipient phase would be the establishment of a free trade association, an example of which would be the contemporary World Trade Organization (discussed in following chapters). A General Agreement on Tariffs and Trade provides the guidelines and equities required to encourage international trade and commerce. A World Bank facilitates the exchange of currencies and provides a degree of stability between international currency values. Enhanced economic integration would occur when certain goods, commodities, or services were given duty-free status characteristic of a customs union. A more advanced stage of integration would involve the creation of a true global common market where goods, capital, and labor could move freely, subject to the laws and taxes of the host nation. Finally, a global economic union would reflect the degree of integration characteristic of the developing European Union previously mentioned.

Experience already indicates, however, that the developing global economy will not reflect the phases and characteristics of the regionally integrated economies. Rather, those regionally integrated markets or unions will preserve their basic integrity and the regional entities will become units of the international economy on the order of a federation of regional economies. That is at least one scenario for future development. Other options, ranging from a global union to complete anarchy, are always possible. The regional economies are in various stages of development, and the world economy, such as it is, is fluid—particularly since the collapse of the Soviet system.

Regional economic associations have long existed, and they have historically changed their shape and form; but in modern times, until the post–World War II era, any economic integration or associations were always sublimated to the integrity of the nation-state. Now integration and cooperation have begun to displace the fierce competitiveness of the traditional nation-state. The global units that appear to have developed a degree of economic affiliation or identity in the post–World War II era include Europe, Eastern Europe, Southeast Asia, India and the subcontinent, China, North America, Latin America, Russia, Japan, the Middle East (OPEC), and possibly the Arctic nation-states, including Norway, Finland, Canada, the state of Alaska, and Siberia. African nations may have an affiliation, but there is little evidence of economic integration. Many of the units interact with other units, and the nation-states within them may have affiliations with yet other regional economic units.

A careful construction of the history of economic developments since World War II suggests the drift toward the creation of a global federation of more or less integrated regional economic systems. Elements of those structures even by 1960 had become sufficient to justify discussion of a global economy and of the role and scope of the United States within such an economy. In addition to the foreign aid, American military expenditures abroad and American business expansion—particularly that relating to agriculture and energy— were the catalysts in global economic expansion between 1950 and 1973.

Chapter 3

THE AMERICAN HEGEMONY
1950–1970

U.S. trade, U.S. business expansion, and U.S. military spending largely defined the economic welfare of the developing regional economies in the free world in the two decades between 1950 and 1970. The Marshall Plan, Japan's Constitution, the North Atlantic Treaty Organization (NATO), and to a lesser extent the Southeast Asia Treaty Organization (SEATO) were important building blocks in the construction of the new world order in the West. But the business of America abroad in the two decades following 1950 had to do more with the sale of American agricultural commodities, the supply and maintenance of vast overseas military forces, and the search for and development of gas and petroleum reserves. Travel, trade, and technology became increasingly important elements of American business abroad.

INTERNATIONAL TRADE

The world, and prominently the Western world, experienced a massive and unparalleled expansion in global trade in the decades after 1950. That trade was both a contributor to and an indicator of the growing strength and size of global productivity. The value of exports increased from $62 billion in 1950 to more than $310 billion in 1970. During those two decades the United States accounted for a remarkably stable 15 percent of total world trade. The European Community's portion of world trade rose from 15 percent in 1950 to almost 28 percent in 1970, with nearly one-half of the total trade volume in 1970 being exports by member nations to other European Community members. The Soviet Union, China, and other communist nations accounted for 9 to 13 percent of total world trade during those 20 years, with most of that being among communist bloc nations. The United Kingdom's share of world trade declined from about 10 percent to 6 percent, and Japan's rose from 1 to 6 percent, increasing at an average annual rate of 19 percent. The share of world trade that less developed nations contributed declined from 33 percent to 19 percent. During these same years, the world's GNP rose fivefold, from $0.7 trillion to $3.2 trillion. Much of the increase in world trade between 1950 and 1970 is accounted for by the sale of manufactured goods, services, and technology. The world's basic business had largely to do with petroleum, iron and steel, aircraft, and food and fiber.

As time passed, the mix of American exports shifted from comprising mostly manufactured goods and agricultural products to services and technology. Generally, the United States enjoyed a favorable balance of trade in the two decades between 1950 and 1970; that is, the United States exported more than it imported. Nevertheless, in most of the years before 1970, with few exceptions, the United States ran a balance-of-payments deficit, spending more abroad than earned from trade. The difference in earnings and expenditures is accounted for by American capital investments and for the most part by American military expenditures abroad. Net U.S. military expenditures abroad rose from about $0.6 billion in 1950 to $3.4 billion in 1970.

Foreign aid under the Marshall Plan and other programs stood at about $3.8 billion in 1970, a level near that of 1950. Unlike military expenditures, foreign economic aid expenditures were usually offset by direct purchases of U.S. goods and services and by the repayment of principal and interest due on U.S. loans using foreign aid funds. Economists tend to agree that foreign aid funds did not contribute significantly to the prevailing balance-of-payments deficit experienced by the United States. Foreign aid under such programs as PL 480 helped others help themselves, while creating markets for U.S. goods and commodities.

Interestingly, the annual net cost of Americans for travel abroad began to rival the annual deficit in military expenditures by 1970. One of the great revolutions in the American experience had to do with the great increase in world travel. While Americans had always been known as a people on the move, the move historically had been westward and internal. Now, Americans began to move into the world, as businesspeople and as travelers and tourists. Tourism and world travel became major new industries in the postwar world. Net expenditures for travel by Americans rose from $0.4 billion in 1950, to $2.3 billion by 1970—and kept rising. Those costs represented more than a drain on the U.S. balance of trade, but also testified to the more worldly view of Americans. That worldly view, in turn, helped inspire overseas American business and military involvement.

AMERICAN AGRICULTURAL EXPORTS

Historically, through the nineteenth century, American agricultural products accounted for the largest share of American exports. Cotton, wheat, rice, corn, and beef products accounted for most agricultural exports. Not until the 1920s did the sale of manufactured products abroad exceed the value of agricultural products sold abroad. Following World War II, American agriculture entered its most productive era. Agricultural prices had collapsed in 1921, and farm prices remained depressed until World War II. Price controls and shortages continued to repress agricultural production. Following the end of the war American agriculture made a spectacular conversion from "horse-and-mule farming" to mechanized, scientific agriculture.

Agricultural production increased 19 percent between 1950 and 1970, even while the number of agricultural workers declined by more than 50 percent. New crops such as soybeans; a modern poultry industry; improved cattle and hog breeds; genetically improved varieties of wheat, cotton, rice, and corn; more fertilizers; and antibiotics and improved veterinary practices all expanded agricultural production. The value of agricultural exports more than doubled from about $3.2 billion annually to more than $7 billion, even while the wholesale prices of farm products declined. Farmers produced considerably larger crops on fewer acres and received lower per unit prices. Production could have reached considerably greater volumes given more favorable marketing conditions, but acreage controls, production quotas, and price supports implemented during the depression remained in place.

Government price support programs continued to generate farm surpluses. The Korean War temporarily reduced surpluses, but by 1956 farm surpluses stored in government warehouses reached an alarming $8.3 billion in value. Congress approved the Agricultural Trade Development and Assistance Act (PL 480) in 1954, which was designed to reduce farm surpluses, provide food for the hungry, and create greater stability in developing areas of the world. Title I of the program provided for the sale of American farm products to other nations in their own currencies, with the proviso that the receipts could be spent only in that country. It provided American foreign aid and somewhat reduced American farm surpluses. Titles II and III allowed the government to distribute stored surpluses for disaster or emergency relief, and Title IV, enacted in 1961, made low-interest American loans available to foreign nations that would use the money to purchase American food products. PL 480 resulted in the government subsidizing the annual sale of approximately $7 billion in American agricultural goods abroad between 1960 and 1970 at a cost of about $1.0 billion annually. Nevertheless, farm prices remained low. The U.S. government became more involved in assisting and stimulating international trade through direct subsidies, foreign loans, and by providing marketing assistance, information, trade missions, and contract services.

Congress approved a "Soil Bank" program in 1956 that resulted in retiring some 28.7 million acres of land from production by 1960. Despite the program, farm surpluses and low farm prices continued. One product of low farm prices during the expansionist phase of American and world economic growth between 1950 and 1970 was to enable American families to spend an increasingly smaller percentage of their income on basic food and fiber and a larger percentage on housing, appliances, automobiles, travel, and other goods and services. At least to a small extent, American agricultural productivity provided similar benefits to some foreign peoples, although most nations of Europe and Southeast Asia vigorously protected their agricultural producers from lower cost American products. Yet another result of American agricultural productivity was that by the mid-1970s American agricultural exports rivaled and on occasion exceeded the value of manufactured products. By then American manufactures faced strong competition from Japan and Europe.

THE ENERGY INDUSTRIES

American interests in overseas oil exploration basically began after World War I. In 1919, predictions of domestic oil shortages, the apparent failure to locate new reserves, and concerns that the United States might be frozen out of overseas opportunities by aggressive British and French petroleum competitors created an oil panic that led American petroleum companies, and particularly Standard Oil of California, into overseas explorations. Turkey, Iraq, Syria, and the Arabian peninsula were areas of particular interest to French and British companies, and Gulf Oil became involved in Turkey, Kuwait, and Bahrain, but withdrew about 1928. American explorations in the 1920s focused on Mexico, Central America, Venezuela, Colombia, the Philippines, and the East Indies. The oil panic died with the discovery of large petroleum reserves in Texas, Oklahoma, and Louisiana in the 1920s, but interest in developing overseas reservoirs remained. Standard Oil of California (SOCAL), for example, assumed Gulf Oil's interests in Bahrain.

In 1933, SOCAL signed an agreement with Saudi Arabia providing for SOCAL's exploration of the eastern half of Saudi Arabia in return for £50,000 cash advance (the pound was then about $3.30), an annual rental fee of £5,000, an additional cash advance of £100,000 upon the discovery of oil, and royalties thereafter at 4 shillings per ton (about .10 cents per barrel). With discoveries in both Bahrain and Saudi Arabia, in 1936 SOCAL recruited the Texas Company (Texaco) for assistance in developing the reserves. Texaco and SOCAL formed a joint subsidiary for production, which later was renamed the Arabian American Oil Company, or ARAMCO. But refining, marketing, and exploration difficulties restrained developments. When World War II erupted, Middle East oil reserves were still largely undiscovered and undeveloped.

The war, however, convinced the United States, which previously felt comfortable as a petroleum exporting nation, that petroleum might be in short supply following the close of hostilities. This regenerated an interest in Middle East petroleum. *In 1948, the United States for the first time became a net importer of oil.* Interest in Middle East and foreign oil explorations rose precipitously thereafter. Unfortunately, Middle East explorations and development confronted enormous political obstacles.

New independent nations and old family and tribal disputes, as well as international rivalries, constantly seemed to thwart development. The Arab-Israeli War of 1948 exacerbated the instability of the region. The 1930s vintage Saudi Arabian ARAMCO petroleum agreements became increasingly important in the amorphous political environment. Standard Oil of New Jersey and Socony Petroleum joined the ARAMCO concession. The ARAMCO partners soon began fighting one another over prices and profits. That conflict produced higher prices for Saudi crude and new conflicts with the Saudi Arabia government over its royalty share, but a remarkable association and liaison between an American company and a strategically situated foreign nation resulted overall.

The ARAMCO–Saudi Arabia petroleum association was one element in the growing involvement by American, British, and French petroleum companies in Middle East oil. Iran, Syria, Iraq, Kuwait, the Independent Emirates, Venezuela, and the Soviet Union, among others, became involved in Middle East oil development and controversy. A critical moment occurred in 1960 when Western nations, including the United States, began lowering the price paid for crude. The response, led by Saudi Arabia's oil minister Abdullah Tariki, was the creation of an international association of oil producers: the Organization of Petroleum Exporting Countries (OPEC).

The original OPEC members included Iraq, Iran, Kuwait, Saudi Arabia, and Venezuela. Its initial objectives were simple: to pressure the oil companies to maintain stable prices, to restore prices to precut levels, and to have the oil companies consult with the OPEC members before making any price changes. Over the next few years, Qatar, Libya, Indonesia, and Abu Dhabi joined OPEC, while negotiations continued between the members and the oil companies (prominently ARAMCO) over prices, the dispensing of royalties, and the elimination of market allowances (that is, discounting from listed prices). The petroleum companies resisted recognizing OPEC's rights to bargain collectively over the issues and preferred unilateral agreements with specific countries. The business issues were intricate, but the overall conflict became identified with the Arab Movement and became politicized in the Middle East and within the Western importing nations. OPEC soon became a significant factor affecting the United States and international trade in general. OPEC signaled the development of a new regional economic entity affecting the global economy. Other such regional federations, less formally constructed, were also in the making.

Although agricultural commodities and petroleum represented the leading edge of the American postwar global trade, the globali-

Global Trade and Technology 43

The OPEC Nations of Africa and the Middle East

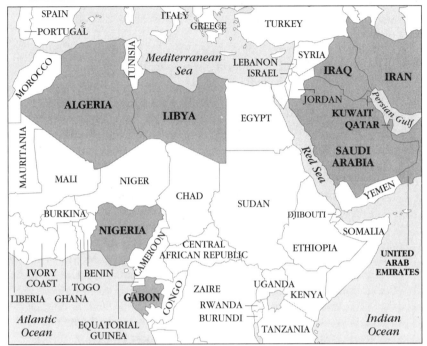

The original OPEC members included Iraq, Iran, Kuwait, Saudi Arabia,
and Venezuela, who were joined by Qatar, Libya, Indonesia, United Arab
Emirates, Nigeria, and Gabon. Other nations have cooperated to a
greater or lessser degree with OPEC efforts to control petroleum
production and prices.

zation of American business after World War II had much to do with
America's past manufacturing strengths: trains, planes, and automobiles, its ubiquitous soft drink and fast foods industries, and its developing technologies related to medicine, aerospace, and computers.

GLOBAL TRADE AND TECHNOLOGY

Globalization was in part a product of technology. Faster travel and
communications compressed the globe. Once distant regions and
nations became contiguous in time and space. The American aircraft

and aerospace industries contributed to a revolution in world travel. During World War II the production of aircraft by American industry soared from a few thousand aircraft per year to 86,000 military planes in 1943 and 110,000 in 1944. Costs declined. A B-24 that cost $238,000 in 1942 was being produced for $137,000 in 1944. When the war ended, America's enormous production capacity withered. The government canceled $21 billion in contracts at the close of hostilities, and the sixty-six aircraft manufacturing plants shrunk to sixteen. The Cold War and the Korean War revived production, but in the mid-1950s the aircraft industry turned with increasing success to civilian design and manufacture.

Within the two decades between 1950 and 1970, the commercial aircraft industry advanced from the propeller reciprocating engine with aircraft speeds of up to 370 miles (600 kilometers) per hour, to the turbopropeller engine with speeds of 500 miles (800 kilometers) per hour, to the turbojet that drove airliners at the speed of sound (and was capable of much more). The first commercial jetliner, the Boeing 707, built in Seattle, Washington, entered service in 1958. Between 1958 and 1970, most commercial carriers made the conversion from propeller-driven to turboprop to turbojet service. European-American air travel, once tedious and circuitous through Newfoundland, Iceland, and Greenland, became direct from New York, Washington, D.C., or Miami to London, Frankfurt, or Paris, and soon, direct flights could be booked from Chicago, Boston, Atlanta, New Orleans, Houston, San Francisco, or Denver to points almost anywhere on Earth.

A major impetus to globalization came from the competitive space programs of the Soviet Union and the United States. Aerospace technology contributed to improvements in commercial air travel and in communications. As then Senator Lyndon Baines Johnson observed, when news of Sputnik I, the Soviet Union's and the world's first artificial satellite, was announced in October 1957, "a new era of history dawned over the world." That era is characterized by the compression of time for travel, of space for communications, and of data for management. The jetliner, communications satellite, and computer were major ingredients in creating the new global economy.

The United States responded to Sputnik by organizing the National Aeronautical and Space Administration (NASA), which began operation in October 1958, one year following the launch of Sputnik. One mission was to create a high-altitude communications relay sta-

Lyndon Baines Johnson
(photo courtesy of NASA)

tion to place an artificial communications satellite into orbit. Two
kinds of satellites were possible: a passive type that would reflect
radio waves or an active type that would receive, amplify, and resend
waves received. The U.S. Navy had already experimented with
bouncing radar waves off of the moon (a passive satellite), and in
1958 the U.S. Army launched an active communications satellite that
among other things broadcast President Dwight D. Eisenhower's
taped Christmas message back to Earth.

NASA launched a reflector balloon satellite in 1960 (Project
Echo) and Relay and Syncom satellites in 1962 and 1963, which
provided active relay capabilities. The big change came with the
launch of two Telstar satellites for American Telephone and Telegraph Company (AT&T) in 1962. The Atlantic cables became history,
and the world became a much more accessible place—for real-time
voice and soon for television communications. A worldwide audi-
ence watched the conclusion of the final Mercury space flight when

Gordon Cooper was recovered at sea from his capsule in May 1963. In 1964, people around the world watched Pope Paul VI tour the Middle East and Olympic athletes compete in Tokyo.

An internationally funded International Telecommunications Satellite Organization (INTELSAT) sponsored the placement by NASA of six INTELSAT satellites between 1962 and 1968, which "provided a global operational network of communications satellites capable of voice (240 channels), television, and teletype facsimile transmissions" between most points on the globe. INTELSAT's operating agency, called COMSAT (the Communications Satellite Corporation), was funded by Congress and directed to develop commercial utilization of the worldwide communications network. Even though NASA communications programs have generally received little attention as compared to the human space-flight programs, the communications programs, at least in the short term, have had a much greater impact in the conduct of life and business on Earth. But the space program in general had a profound influence on life on our planet.

Space stimulated the mind, creating opportunities for invention and for new ways of doing old things. And space had some very real, practical impacts. Space research brought about new materials, resulted in innovative techniques for systems engineering, improved and miniaturized electronic and computer systems, and enhanced medical technology. Space facilitated the creation of real-time communications systems. Space tested new dimensions of the human physiology. Space, in the context of the Cold War, accelerated education in science, mathematics, and engineering, in the United States, the Soviet Union, and throughout the world. Space contributed to broadening our knowledge of the universe, and most significantly to increasing knowledge about the globe and its peoples and to the perception of the "whole" planet Earth.

Upon their first view of Earth from space, many NASA astronauts commented with great passion on the beauty of our world, its possible fragility, and their sense of the oneness of Earth and its inhabitants. The Apollo 17 view of our planet taken from near the moon is one of the most published photographs in the world. Perhaps even more profound is "Earthrise," the photograph of the Earth rising over the moon's horizon. The photographs, as do the comments of the astronauts, speak volumes about the changing perception people have of their planet and of themselves. Ours became a global community. The United States became part of a global economy.

Only within the past half-century have Americans become conscious of the rain forests of South and Central America and the potential decline of whale and seal populations in the oceans. The hole in the ozone layer, indeed the concept of an ozone layer, are recent perceptions. Famine in Ethiopia, ethnic wars in Rwanda, crop failures in China, fuel shortages in England, apartheid in South Africa, and revolutions in Grenada now have real-time consequences in the United States. Before World War II, and before the entry into space, knowledge of the world about us was limited, but, more critically, information and knowledge were dated. Today our knowledge of events around the world is real-time, first-person, hands-on knowledge transmitted in audio and video image by real-time fixed Earth-orbit satellite communications systems. The world is much smaller, more integrated, and more interdependent, socially, environmentally, and economically.

INTELSAT is a worldwide network of communications satellites that link some 140 countries. Television programs from throughout the United States and the world can be brought into virtually every home. Navigation satellites provide accurate locations for ships, aircraft, and even individuals anywhere on Earth. Resource satellites, many using infrared scanning technology, provide reliable global information on crops and forest resources and on mineral and water sources. Weather satellites provide highly accurate information on weather conditions, storms, and rainfall throughout the world. Military and spy satellites can locate threatening missile sites, arms, shipping, and personnel movements. Space research satellites such as the Hubble telescope provide new vistas for solar system and celestial studies. Space laboratories offer the prospect of producing new materials or of producing existing materials such as crystals more effectively and cheaply than can be accomplished on Earth. Computers, at home and in the workplace, and now network systems such as Internet, help facilitate the acquisition, management, and effective use of the deluge of new information.

Humankind has thus experienced a different kind of revolution. There have been relatively few epochs in human history in which change has been so profound as in our own time. The discovery of fire, the inception of agriculture, the invention of writing, the development of gunpowder, the utilization of time, the acceptance of the Copernican theory that Earth evolved about the sun—all brought similar disturbances, disruptions, advances, and change to human life—but those changes occurred geographically and incrementally over hundreds or thousands of years. What has changed in the past half-century is the pace of change itself and the universality of change. It is difficult for any society to ignore, be unaffected by, or to reject change. Change has become a real-time, global phenomenon. The essence of that change is technological innovation and invention.

Invention occurs when novelty in thought incites action. That is, one must not only have a new idea, but that idea must also be effected by action or creation. Technology is, in fact, the application of an idea or knowledge. New technology is the product of invention. The process of invention, according to Abbot Payson Usher, author of the classic *History of Mechanical Inventions,* involves first a synthesis of familiar ideas and knowledge and the perception of an incomplete pattern or need—that is, the realization that a problem exists. There is no opportunity for invention until someone realizes that there might be a better, more efficient, less expensive, or faster way to open a soft drink can than with the existing can openers—or, better yet, how does one open a can when no can opener is available? Not only must a problem be realized, but second, there must be a fortuitous configuration of thought or events that offers a solution to a problem. That could be a physicist with an interest in metallurgy, a tailor sewing a zipper, or simply someone in a workshop who is curious. The third step is the insight, the inception of the idea, the act of invention. Perhaps scoring the metal and using a lever to break it from the top would open the can. Finally, there must be a critical revision and mastery of the invention. The lever or tab should fit the finger. The scoring should be in such a way as to prevent cuts to the skin or lips. Thus, somehow, emerges the pull-tab can opener.

The point is that the more information available, and the more receptive people are to whom it is available, the more likely is there to be invention. The communications revolution simply creates the greater likelihood of a problem being recognized and increases the probability of inception of an idea to solve the problem. Advances in communications, via satellite, computers, radio, and the press, have increased the probability of new ideas and invention. While the invention curve has been accelerated within the past fifty years as never before in world history it may likely flatten somewhat as the world absorbs the information that has been around, but not truly available. Improved communications does not create information but rather makes information more available.

The greatest beneficiary of this new information age has been the economy; that is the collective actions and decisions that produce goods and services and determine how well or how poorly we live. What has happened is that increasingly "the economy" includes the world, not just the United States, or the United States and the Western nations. The world has become a much smaller, more integrated, more complex system than it was even half a century ago. The old spatial concepts of geopolitics have been massively revised. Space (in the linear geophysical sense) and control over that space is no longer equivalent to "world power." But space beyond the atmosphere and the utilization of space beyond the Earth is becoming critical to the welfare of those on the Earth. The "world city," Europe, is no longer distant from the once "peripheral" lands. Johann Heinrich von Thunen, a geographer, identified the huge, non-contiguous urban-industrial complex in northwestern Europe and northeastern Anglo-America as a global economic core region that arose about 1750 and has since shaped world economic development. Radiating from that core were economic zones, largely agricultural, with the zones of most intense application of labor nearest the world city, and the least developed zones, such as the rangeland and forests, most remote from the world city. With human ascent into space, the world city had effactually become Earth. There were no peripheral lands. The environment was becoming a "whole Earth" environment and the economy a global economy. Humans scattered throughout the globe began to have a real-time connection and association with one another. Time and distance were being compressed.

As it began to emerge, the global economy retained a strong regional and hemispheric configuration. The two hemispheres were roughly the East and the West—the communist and the free world. The Soviet Union maintained economic and military dominance in the East, stretching from its western perimeter that looped from the Baltic Sea through Berlin into the Adriatic Sea and eastward through Eastern Europe to the Pacific, and then southward through China into Vietnam, Laos, and Cambodia. Within this vast system, China and Southeast Asia comprised autonomous regional economies and military powers. Eastern Europe retained a degree of regional economic integrity, but little political autonomy.

The West included Western Europe from the Straits of Gibraltar northward to the Arctic Ocean, Great Britain, the nations bordering the Mediterranean, North America, and the Pacific Rim countries

The Eagle returns to the Command Space Module following the historic landing on the lunar surface by astronauts Neil A. Armstrong and Edwin E. Aldrin, Jr., in July 1969. Michael Collins was aboard the Command Space Module in orbit about the moon. Smyth's Sea is the large dark-colored area on the lunar surface. Earth rises above the lunar horizon. If not Sputnik, certainly the flight of Apollo 11 marked a "new era of history." Humankind began to perceive itself as a part of a new global community.

including Japan, South Korea, Thailand, Burma, and India, with the Philippines and Australia. Within this conglomerate the United States held economic and military hegemony.

This, of course, is a very simplistic overview. It does suggest, however, that the world was largely divided into two economic spheres, representing euphemistically the East and the West. The remaining "nonaligned nations," prominently South America and Africa, were strongly influenced by the economic and political pressures of the Cold War and tended to be economically dependent upon one or the other world powers.

Within the Western sphere, as Europe and Japan recovered from the economic devastation of World War II, each began building a regional economy that would become increasingly competitive with the United States. In addition, the eastern Mediterranean (OPEC) nations achieved a strong measure of regional economic integrity by virtue of their asserting control over their energy resources. By 1973, U.S. hegemony over trade and finance in the Western world no longer existed. But the three dominant regional Western economies, the United States, Japan, and the United Kingdom–Europe tended to subordinate their competitive interests and conflicts to the greater goal of maintaining Western economic and military solidarity to counter the Soviet-China communist bloc. Both the Soviet and the U.S. economic spheres contained growing regional economic federations that could and did challenge the dominance respectively of the Soviet Union and the United States. Indeed, the nation-state that had been the basic unit of global economic activity for 500 years was being supplanted by something new: regional economic federations that interacted on a global sphere.

Chapter 4

AGRICULTURE AND AUTOMOBILES

In the quarter-century following the Marshall Plan (1948–1973), there was a dramatic shift in world economic power. The United States became the business and financial epicenter of the world. It was a role largely cast upon the United States by default rather than the initiative and planning of American business and financial leaders. Indeed, had the American people been aware of the evolving role of the United States in the world economy, many, if not most, in 1945 or 1950 would likely have objected. The quantitative leap in American economic power came in part because most of the world's money had taken refuge in American banks during the war. In addition, because much of the world's agricultural and manufacturing capacity was damaged, destroyed, or otherwise out of production, the United States became the major supplier of the world's food, fiber, raw materials, iron and steel manufactured products, petroleum, machinery, and capital. Most important, after World War II U.S. agricultural and industrial production rose dramatically.

In each year between 1950 and 1970, the value of American exports exceeded the value of imports. Exports rose in every category. The value of agricultural exports, long a U.S. staple in world trade, rose precipitously in the postwar years. The value of wheat and wheat flour exports, for example, rose from the $25 million per year averaged in the 1930s and through the war years to exceed $1 billion annually in every year between 1960 and 1970. Receipts from

American raw cotton exports were generally double or triple their prewar levels through the mid-1960s, but began a precipitous decline about 1965. Between 1950 and 1970 annual tobacco exports generally exceeded by three or four times their prewar levels. Farm production and domestic consumption of farm products rose even more dramatically as the United States experienced the "Great Agricultural Revolution."

The United States expanded its traditional role as a world supplier of raw materials and crude food products even while becoming the world's major supplier of manufactured products. By 1970 the value of exported semi-manufactured products were at about 600 percent of 1950 levels, and manufactured exports had increased five-fold. Between 1950 and 1970 the United States provided most of the world's iron and steel products including automobiles, parts, engines, aircraft, and weapons. Exports of automobiles, engines, and parts had exceeded $500 million only in 1928 and 1929. From 1950 through 1970 the value of such exports rose from about $1 billion to in excess of $3 billion annually. Whereas U.S. exports of machine tools and machinery had previously been negligible, the value of such exports soared during the war and continued to rise from $2 billion in 1950 to $11.7 billion by 1970. In many respects, the changes in American agriculture were greater than those in industry.

The American military and American diplomacy and overseas diplomatic posts became important adjuncts to the "Rise to Globalism." The annual defense budget rose from prewar levels of $500 million or less to $300 billion or more. Despite the U.S.'s greater military and economic power, the nation seemed to be more vulnerable that ever before. Military and productive power had its limits. As diplomatic historian Stephen Ambrose commented, "Six percent of the world's people could not run the lives of the remaining 94 percent." That six percent, however, could and did markedly affect the way the other 94 percent lived.

The shift to globalism and the spectacular growth of American economic power were less the products of forethought and planning and more the result of transformations in the American economy. Americans were generally preoccupied with supplying the burgeoning domestic markets with food, clothing, shelter, highways, automobiles, radios, television sets, and appliances. American agriculture became a wholly different social and productive system after World War II.

THE GREAT AMERICAN AGRICULTURAL REVOLUTION

During the half-century following World War II, American agriculture substituted technology and science for people. As a result, farm production rose from approximately $10 billion annually to $50 billion by 1990, while farm populations declined precipitously. Farm population declined from about 20 percent to 2 percent of total population between 1945 and 1995 as people moved from the farm to the city, and the United States became a distinctively urban society.

Changes in agricultural productivity, stimulated by technological advances begun perhaps a hundred years earlier by Cyrus McCormick (inventor of the reaper) and John Deere (inventor of the steel moldboard plow), among others, became a revolution under the impetus of mechanization after World War II. Although steam tractors were introduced in the nineteenth century, and internal combustion farm tractors in the early twentieth, mechanized agriculture became a reality only after World War II, as farmers invested their profits (which had been virtually nonexistent during the extended agricultural depression that lasted from 1921 through 1940) in tractors and equipment. Between 1945 and 1970, for example, numbers of tractors on farms rose from a few hundred thousand to more than five million, averaging more than one tractor per farm. The number of grain combines on farms jumped from about two hundred thousand to one million. Cotton, which was wholly hand harvested in 1945, by 1970 was 96 percent machine harvested. The introduction of hybrid grains, improved chemical fertilizers and pesticides, better management practices, and the consolidation of farms into larger and more efficient units, coupled with federal farm programs that provided price guarantees and marketing assistance, all stimulated greater production and higher yields.

By 1970, as American economic influence in the global economy seemed to wane under the competition of a stronger European Common Market and rising Japanese manufactured exports, American agricultural production became relatively more important in world markets and began to constitute a greater percentage of total U.S. export income, with agricultural goods, on occasion, exceeding the value of American manufactured exports. War in Vietnam, energy shortages, and the OPEC embargo (mentioned in the previous chapter) created an economic crisis in the world and in the United States—of which American agriculture was a prime beneficiary. In the 1970s, American agripower began to be used as an instrument of national policy in an effort to maintain the U.S. economic and military hegemony in the world. Indeed American agriculture helped establish that hegemony in the first place.

The great American agricultural revolution had an enormous impact on extending the American presence in the global community after World War II. Even though the United States had long supplied commodities such as wheat, corn, cotton, and tobacco to international markets, after the war the world became increasingly dependent on U.S. agricultural products, particularly on grain. The account by Dan Morgan, a business historian and journalist, of the *Merchants of Grain* (1979) describes the entry of the U.S. merchant into the international grain trade and how following World War II that trade became integral to the nation's stature as a global economic power.

The United States emerged from World War II as an agricultural superpower. Few countries of Asia or Europe could produce grain in sufficient quantities for export. The United States supplied fully one half of the world's available supply of wheat between 1945 and 1949. The United Nations Relief and Rehabilitation Agency (UNRRA) provided emergency relief supplies of grain to hungry peoples in China, Japan, Hungary, the Philippines, Austria, and around the world. General Douglas MacArthur began importing wheat to Japan in 1946 to feed school children and civilians. Japanese consumption of wheat rose from an average of 30 pounds to 90 pounds per person by 1955. Similarly, Chiang Kai-shek welcomed American relief shipments of wheat to China after the close of hostilities, thus beginning the "Americanization" of the Asian diet. European nations used Marshall Plan funds to purchase wheat, rice, and soybeans from American producers. As the affluence of European and Asian nations grew, the peoples of those countries added more wheat and meat to their diets. In the early years, the lack of capital more than anything else prevented foreign nations from purchasing sufficient quantities of American grain to stem the growth of large domestic surpluses.

In 1954, Congress approved PL 480, which released federal farm surpluses for school lunches, relief agencies, and for sale to foreign countries in their own currencies to be spent only in those countries. PL 480 combined U.S. diplomatic and market interests under a broad humanitarian umbrella. Food for peace, agricultural assistance to underdeveloped nations, famine relief, and international financing fell into place under PL 480.

Foreign purchases under PL 480 involved a request by a foreign government to the U.S. government to purchase U.S. grain, paid for by a U.S. government loan (to be repaid by the purchasing nation in its own currency for exclusive use by the United States within that country). Payments for the shipments went from the U.S. Treasury to commercial banks in the United States and from the bank to the private exporter. The U.S. government became the principal financier of world grain trade. That financing and trade helped establish the American economic hegemony in a world often starving or on the brink of starvation. It relieved the growing crop surpluses accumulating in the U.S., relieved hunger and thus staved off unrest that might precipitate a communist takeover in nonaligned nations, and helped satisfy an American sense of morality and humanitarianism.

AMERICAN GRAIN MERCHANTS GO GLOBAL

Although American merchants had a history of global trade in agricultural commodities—cotton, tobacco, wheat, and rice—in the twentieth century American grain merchants had generally relinquished international trade to European firms. Minneapolis became the center of American milling in the late nineteenth century with the introduction of chilled steel rollers for milling that replaced the old pounding mills and the development of purifying systems that left a high-grade white flour. Cadwallader Washburn, the founder of what would become General Mills, and Charles Alfred Pillsbury, of Pillsbury flour fame, pioneered in the development of modern milling techniques. Grain merchants such as Will Cargill and Frank Peavey became the connecting links between the farmer and the mills. They bought grain, stored it in elevators along the railroad lines, and sold and shipped the grain to the mills. They were the buyers, the shippers, and the handlers—the "merchants of grain." They developed banking associations and alliances with railroads. James J. Hill, owner of the Great Northern and Northern Pacific Railroads, provided transportation and financing for the grain crops and reaped great profits from both. Grain merchants at first bought directly from the farmer and sold directly to the mills, but as time passed they bought and sold more and more of their grain through the established commodity markets such as the Chicago Board of Trade.

Shortly after the turn of the century, and following the death of its founder Will Cargill, Cargill Company survived on the edge of bankruptcy because of bad investments in railroads and irrigation systems in Montana, made by his son, William. About the time of World War I, and concurrent with the spectacular leap in grain prices caused by the outbreak of hostilities, John MacMillan, the son-in-law of Will Cargill, seized control from William and began converting the firm from essentially a regional brokerage firm into a national dealer.

In the 1920s, Cargill expanded its operations throughout the United States and into Canada and Argentina. The expansion was in part designed to meet the growing competition from European merchants. Grain shortages caused by World War I brought European grain dealers to the United States as never before. Continental Grain Company, established by Jules and Louis Freibourg in France in 1921, began buying grain elevators and establishing offices in the United States. The Bunge firm, established in Holland by Charles Bunge in the early nineteenth century, became a major contender for grain in the American markets. Edouard and Ernesto Bunge refocused the firm from its traditional general merchandise business to specialize in grain. Ernesto Bunge moved to Argentina in 1876 and established an affiliate, Bunge y Born, in that country. Although less aggressive than Continental Grain, Bunge began buying American grain elevators after World War I. Similarly, the Dreyfus firm, established by Leopold Louis-Dreyfus in Basel, Switzerland, in 1852, established a stronger presence in American grain markets in the 1920s. Pillsbury and General Mills as well moved more heavily into the grain and elevator business, but primarily to supply their own mills.

The financial collapse ensuing from the Great Depression forced a retrenchment of the activities of the grain merchants until the outbreak of World War II. During that time Cargill expanded its basic transportation and storage systems. The war in Europe, with the exclusion of European competitors, left Cargill the dominant player in the American grain trade, but that trade was largely channeled through government purchases. Until 1945, American milling and grain marketing had been largely domestic oriented. After World War II that began to change when American firms such as Cargill went global. While their European counterparts, Bunge, Continental, and Dreyfus, enjoyed a history of international trade, American firms entering the foreign arena in the post–World War II era, whether in grain, energy, soft drinks, or electronics, faced a strange and difficult new environment.

Cargill moved slowly but resolutely into the world arena. In 1945, Cargill acquired Nutrena Mills and went into corn and soybean processing. A year later, Cargill, in association with the International Basic Economy Corporation, began building grain elevators in Brazil. Next, the company built a large grain elevator near Quebec, Canada, and in 1955 organized Tradax, Inc., an independent grain company in Geneva, Switzerland. American expansion into the international grain trade, however, was inextricably linked to the U.S. government and its policy interests. PL 480 made Cargill and other American grain merchants partners in the distribution of American farm commodities. Food and grain became closely linked with diplomacy, federal financial policies and programs, federal farm programs, federal extension and educational programs, and to an extent, United Nations programs and aspirations. The connection between government and industry was perhaps particularly evident in the American rice industry, which had a long history and tradition of international trade.

THE AMERICAN RICE INDUSTRY

Until recent years, the United States has historically sold most of the rice it produces overseas, accounting for 15 to 30 percent of the world's exports. Rice is an agribusiness with historic international dimensions. U.S. production began in 1685 and averaged 3 million pounds annually in the eighteenth century. During the antebellum years, rice exports from South Carolina and Georgia were valued at $150 million annually. In the late nineteenth century, production shifted to the coastal prairies of Louisiana and Texas and in the early twentieth century began in Arkansas and California. In the post–World War II era, American rice sales netted $1 billion or more annually. Rice, perhaps more so than wheat and corn, became an important element in the extension of American Cold War diplomacy.

Between 1950 and 1960 acreage planted in rice jumped from 1.6 to 2.6 million acres. Rice production spread rapidly in California, and Mississippi joined the lists as a major producer of rice. Grain combines, improved systems of aeration and drying, better ginning equipment, and fertilization, seeding, and insect control by aircraft, as well as the introduction of new, higher yielding, and more disease-resistant plant varieties stimulated even greater production. During the Korean War the U.S. government and the United Nations absorbed large quantities of U.S. rice, most of which was directed to

Southeast Asia. Rice farmers generally ignored Agricultural Stabilization and Conservation (ASC) program allotments and price supports
between 1949 and 1954, planting larger acreages than allotted under
the federal farm program. Harvests from acreage planted in excess of
the allotments disqualified the farmer from price supports, but if
prices exceeded support levels, as they generally did, the farmer
profited considerably. The disruption of Asian production and marketing caused by the collapse of Nationalist China and the Korean
War created rising demands and rising prices for American rice. But
in 1954, with the end of the Korean War, prices collapsed and government granaries absorbed 26.7 million hundredweight of carry-
over rice for storage. In 1955, rice acreage allotments were cut by
almost 25 percent. Nevertheless, despite erratic and cyclical demand, over the long term rice production and sales continued
to rise.

Even as government programs were reducing the supply of rice,
world and domestic demand for American rice rose. In 1955, the
United States accounted for 7 percent of the world trade in rice. By
1970, the United States was selling 20 percent of the world's rice.
Incongruously, the government talked free markets but maintained
strong production and marketing controls. Federal agencies became
ever-larger buyers of American rice even while farm programs re-
strained production. And government-funded research and experiment stations constantly promoted higher crop yields even while the
farm programs sought to curb production through acreage allotments. Exports were usually handled by direct mill orders and, because of technical flaws in PL 480 specifications, generally sold
outside of PL 480 markets. Much of the American rice crop was
handled by a relatively small number of firms, often representing
hundreds of growers. Major firms or associations included the Arkansas Rice Growers' Cooperative Association, the California Rice Growers' Association, and Louisiana State Rice Milling Company (later
Riviana Foods). American Rice, Inc., was a centralized rice milling
and marketing cooperative serving approximately 1800 rice farmers
in the Gulf Coast area of Texas and Louisiana. Ralph S. Newman, then
(1981) president of American Rice, Inc., described the American rice
industry as an international agribusiness preoccupied with overseas
events. It is also, he said, a business that is "affected, dominated,
regulated, and influenced by Washington."

The infrastructure of the rice industry extended from the board
rooms of rice milling companies and agricultural cooperatives into
the offices of government agencies and congressmen. In the 1960s

and 1970s in particular, influential senators such as Allen J. Ellender of Louisiana, Senator J. W. Fulbright of Arkansas, and Senator James Eastland of Mississippi championed the cause of rice in Congress. These senators and others in government agricultural programs assisted in redefining PL 480 policies so as to facilitate better overseas rice marketing. For example, India agreed to buy one million tons of American rice for each of the four years between 1960 and 1964 using PL 480 loans. The United States lost the important Cuban market in 1960, but obtained large export (PL 480) contracts with South Korea, Indonesia, Vietnam, Iraq, and Saudi Arabia. Sales to the European Economic Community, South Africa, the United Kingdom, and South America rose steadily through the 1960s. By 1966 the United States was exporting more than 1.5 million metric tons of rice and soon surpassed Thailand as the world's leading rice-exporting nation. Indeed, between 1960 and 1965, sales of U.S. farm produce abroad totaled $25 billion, of which $583 million was accounted for by rice sales. By 1973, foreign sales of rice exceeded $1 billion annually.

THE AMERICAN INFRASTRUCTURE FOR FOREIGN AGRICULTURAL TRADE

The improved export situation in the 1960s and following had much to do with a closer collaboration and association between government agencies and agribusiness. The infrastructure of rice, wheat, cotton, tobacco, and indeed of much of American agriculture extended from the farm to the House and Senate. It included farmer associations, the agricultural colleges, agricultural experiment stations, the Agricultural Extension Service, and the Agricultural Stabilization and Conservation Service (established in 1961 to supplant the old depression-era Agricultural Adjustment Administration [AAA]).

Overseas marketing connections and associations, in addition to the private ones developed by producers and mills, included the USDA Foreign Agricultural Service (FAS) established in 1930 "to assist American farmers in adjusting their operations and practices to meet world competition and demand for farm products." In the post–World War II era the FAS developed a global information network that provided data and analyses of worldwide agricultural production, trade, marketing, prices, and consumption. The service maintained market development offices in what was then West Germany, Belgium, Switzerland, the United Kingdom, and South Africa and collected information from U.S. embassies and consulates throughout the world. The Diplomatic Corps (often consular officials and staff) also provided worldwide information on crops, weather, imports, and exports. This information, and other domestic data (including information from the Bureau of the Census) was also evaluated by the USDA Economic Research Service and passed to interested parties. Thus, nominally *private* international trade and commerce developed a close interface with government.

MANUFACTURING AND THE WORLD MARKET

American agriculture adapted itself more easily to the world marketplace than did manufacturing in the decade of the 1960s. That was true in part because a—if not *the*—major market for American agricultural products had always been abroad. On the other hand, most American manufactures, and prominently automobiles, tractors, household appliances, and farm implements, had since the turn of the century been absorbed in the domestic market. And that market had continued uninterrupted growth until the advent of the depression and World War II. The end of the war and the destruction of manufacturing plants in Europe and Asia created tremendous new market opportunities for American manufacturers that had not previously existed. But the pent-up demands of the domestic market were even greater than international opportunities.

Although many companies made entries into the international market between 1950 and 1960, according to Ira Magaziner and Robert Reich (*Minding America's Business,* 1983), they discovered their international ventures were less profitable than opportunities in the United States. In addition, by the 1960s, European industrial-based economies in particular were regaining their prewar capabilities. Japan's industrial capacity grew at an even more rapid rate. European markets were increasingly being shielded with protectionist policies by governments anxious to rebuild their industrial power base. In addition, Japan's domestic market was virtually closed to American manufacturers. That condition, combined with the reality that profits were higher, risks lower, and competition less keen—and that American manufacturers historically focused on the domestic market— helped discourage American manufacturers from international competition. As Magaziner and Reich indicated:

The large U.S. domestic market is the envy of every company in Europe. Without venturing beyond U.S.borders, most U.S. companies can gain a huge market base over which to amortize fixed costs and the costs of research and development. They can build world-scale plants, and gain considerable experience in a business, without having to challenge export markets.

The results, however, were a mixed blessing, for U.S. companies became less aggressive abroad.

Disposable personal income rose by 2.5 times the 1950 level in the United States, even while populations rose from 150 to 203 million in 1970. During these decades, and for many of the years following, much of the world's marketplace was in fact in the United States. Rather than attempting to market goods abroad in the more competitive and less profitable world marketplace in the decade of the 1960s, American industry began to manufacture goods abroad for sale in the United States. Labor and raw materials remained generally less expensive overseas than in the United States through most of the remaining years of the century. Thus while American manufacturers became international in the postwar era, their trade tended to remain domestic, that is, United States directed. Internationalization meant a relocation of American capital abroad, rather than a redirection of American marketing. Savings and more efficient production was also achieved by merging U.S. manufactures with European industries, thus increasing productive capacity and giving those foreign firms better access to American markets. Not only, of course, were American manufacturers directing their market energies toward the mammoth American marketplace, but the reemerging and the newly developed industries of the industrial world did so as well.

THE AUTOMOTIVE INDUSTRY

The import and export of U.S. automotive parts and vehicles between 1950 and 1970 illustrates the changing character of both production and marketing in the American automotive industry. Between 1950 and 1960 the value of automotive vehicles, parts, and engines exported from the United States rose from $746 million to $1.3 billion, while total new and used car sales in the United States rose from $10 to $17 billion. It was easy to see where American automotive manufacturers focused their energies. Imports of foreign automotive vehicles, parts, and engines in the same ten years increased from $23 to $633 million. At the close of the decade in 1960, U.S. auto manufacturers enjoyed trade surplus of more than $600 million. A good portion of the automotive sales to the United States were accounted for by the popular Volkswagen import from West Germany and by luxury automobiles from West Germany and the United Kingdom. These imports, for the most part, were considered noncompetitive with mainline American automobiles.

However, by 1967, Americans were importing more cars than they were selling abroad. In the following two decades (1970–1990) not only did the United States lose more of the global automotive market, but American automakers lost more and more of their own domestic market to foreign competition. Although the export of U.S. autos rose from $1.2 to $3.6 billion between 1960 and 1970, imports soared from $633 million to almost $6 billion. Much of the increase came from Japanese imports rather than from Europe. The Honda displaced the Volkswagen in the American market. More critically, the traditional large, heavy, eight cylinder, chromed American sedan lost market share to the small import. The Japanese Honda and Toyota and the West German Audi and Mercedes became mainline in America.

But the sheer size of the American market discouraged automakers from retooling and redesigning their vehicles and from attempting to compete in foreign markets. Even though they might lose market share globally, domestic total sales continued to rise. U.S. auto sales more than doubled from $17 billion to $35 billion between 1960 and 1970. Two-thirds of the U.S. market, without redesigning and retooling, was more profitable than all of it if preserving that market meant heavy new plant investment. Moreover, competition in overseas markets (and in the American import market) meant producing a different product than American auto manufacturers were accustomed to producing. European and Japanese consumers did not favor American-style automobiles. Further discouraging U.S. attempts to compete more strongly in foreign markets was that those overseas markets were much more protected than the U.S. markets. Thus it seemed expedient, at least through the 1970s, for American automakers to concentrate, as they always had, on the traditional domestic market.

Through the 1960s and 1970s the "Big Three" automakers, Chrysler, Ford, and General Motors, offered large, gas-guzzling, expensive vehicles that lacked the quality of many imports. Rather than compete in the small (import) car business, cash-rich American

manufacturers preferred associations or mergers with European automotive companies that could sell their smaller products in the
United States while they could continue to focus on the traditional
lines. There were tentative efforts to reduce production costs at
home by purchasing parts and engines manufactured by lower-paid
overseas workers and by transferring production facilities abroad.
Unions and manufacturers also leaned toward stronger protectionist
policies as Japanese vehicles in particular began to make inroads into
the U.S. auto market. For the most part, despite considerable overseas investments and rising competition, U.S. automakers remained
ambivalent about entering the global economy. That disposition
changed markedly during the last quarter of the twentieth century.

The fortunes and profits of the American auto industry were
inextricably entwined with those of the American steel industry.
Steel too exhibited complacency and a strong provincialism. The
American market was wholly sufficient.

IRON AND STEEL

*From the end of World War II into the late 1950s, American steel
mills could sell all they produced at almost any price. They enjoyed
what economists call an oligopoly, where a few big firms control
the market—and the profits. When steel-workers struck or threatened to strike at the expiration of a contract, the companies, which
were all bound by the same industry-wide labor agreement,
handed out wage increases and benefits that outran all others in
U.S. industry. Then the big steel firms raised prices to whatever
levels were necessary to satisfy profits, stockholder returns, and the
new pay scales.*

—John Strohmeyer, *Crisis in Bethlehem* (1986)

J. Bruce Johnston, executive vice president of U.S. Steel, the
nation's largest steel producer, in 1985 explained that the inception
and growth of U.S. Steel had been due to Andrew Carnegie's insight
and innovation. Before Carnegie, steelmaking was a cottage industry.
The coal mine, the quarry, the furnace, the shipping, and the steelmaking were each separate businesses. Andrew Carnegie put them
all together. He built the world's first integrated steel mill, centered
on the new technology of the Bessemer converter. After that no one
could compete. The new organization and process overnight de-

stroyed the European steel industry and put American steel manufacturers in the driver's seat. What innovation did not do to Europe's steel industry, two world wars in Europe and a depression did. The U.S. iron and steel industry emerged from World War II, like the U.S. automobile industry, as the undisputed leader of the industry. But that leadership did not last for automobiles or for steel.

By the 1960s America's leading steel producers were beginning to feel the bite of competition. European manufacturers staged a remarkable recovery. The inception of the European Economic Union came with the realization of the need for cooperation between France and Germany to provide the coal, iron, and equipment needed to reconstruct the region's basic industry. Japan's steel industry emerged after World War II from being a "nonindustry" to become a major world competitor. Both Europe and Japan enjoyed modern plants and equipment, and they benefited from relatively lower wage rates. There were virtually no iron and steel manufactured imports into the United States before 1958, when the United States consumed approximately $77 million in imported goods. By 1963, U.S. imports reached $598 million, slightly exceeding exports of $505 million. In each year thereafter the United States imported more iron and steel products than it exported, with imports approaching $2 billion in 1970. Nevertheless, as with the automobile industry, it was business as usual for American steel manufacturers whose total sales continued to rise despite foreign competition.

In much the way that automobile manufacturers continued to produce the traditional models, steel manufacturers declined to retool in the face of rising competition from abroad. U.S. Steel and Bethlehem Steel Corporation, America's numbers one and two producers, depended on plant and equipment constructed at the turn of the century. Building new plants, particularly given the rising replacement costs, were deemed prohibitive—and unnecessary.

Economic historian Louis Galambos, commenting on the American steel industry in his study of America in *Middle Age: A New History of the U.S. in the Twentieth Century,* noted that even though U.S. Steel was a large corporation, with assets of about $2 billion, and although it manufactured products "ranging from very fine wire to the largest steel girders," it was focused exclusively on iron and steel. "It would no more have ventured into aluminum production than a normal college professor would have doubled as a race car driver." U.S. Steel, like General Motors, Ford, and Chrysler, had world-class size but more provincial aspirations.

Similarly, author John Strohmeyer, in his personalized and fascinating book *Crisis in Bethlehem,* attributes later problems, indeed crises, in the steel industry to the failure to adopt new and modern manufacturing techniques. Specifically, continuous casting, replacing the older and more costly ingot mold and rolling processes, had been adopted "around the world in the sixties, but not in the American integrated steel industry." Bethlehem Steel, in partnership with Republic, Youngstown, and Inland Steel corporations experimented with the process in the Bethlehem mill in the early 1960s, and while deciding that it was efficient, believed it was costly and unsuitable for high-volume production and thus abandoned the system. Japanese steel producers, meanwhile, "picked up the concept and adopted it for high-volume production."

Subsequently, following a recommendation by an internal research committee, Bethlehem Steel decided to build a continuous casting operation into one of its older and smaller plants at Johnstown, Pennsylvania (despite recommendations by the committee to build at a larger plant in Seattle or Steelton, Pennsylvania). After investing $10 million in the new facility, Bethlehem abandoned the conversion because the Johnstown facility could not effectively contain the new process. The debacle marked the end, for at least several decades, of the modernization of American steel-manufacturing processes. Meanwhile, by 1981, Europe had converted 45 percent of its steel operations to continuous casting and Japan used the system on 70 percent of its production, whereas the United States had only 21 percent of its plant capacity using continuous casting technology. It meant, coupled with existing wage disparities, that Europe and Japan could produce high-quality steel at a considerably lower cost than could the United States.

Although aware of the global competition as early as 1962, the U.S. steel industry continued its pattern of conceding high wage contracts followed by domestic price increases. Between the close of World War II and 1962, steel prices were raised ten times following new labor contracts. Assured that such would not happen following a labor settlement, President John F. Kennedy was shocked when U.S. Steel announced a $6 per ton price increase in April 1962. The nation's twelve largest steel manufacturers followed with identical price increases—including Bethlehem Steel Corporation, whose president only that morning denied that a price increase was in the works, but suggested that steel companies would be trying to lower prices because of competition from foreign sources. Following a dramatic confrontation with the administration, the steel companies rescinded their price increase.

Despite the relatively clear evidence of problems, other than discussion and rhetoric advocating higher tariffs on imported steel and automobiles, nothing changed through the decade of the 1960s. And steel and automobiles continued making money and returning comfortable profits to their stockholders. The percentage of American families owning automobiles rose from 50 percent in 1945 to 82 percent by 1970. One-third of U.S. households owned two or more cars. The previously almost-nonexistent auto insurance business rose from a $1.25 billion industry to a $14.6 billion industry by 1970. The motel (motor-hotel) supplanted the inner-city hotel. The two-car garage, suburban America, shopping centers, and malls were manifestations of the new age of the automobile. Federal, state, and local expenditures for highways rose from $1.2 to $16.7 billion between 1946 and 1970. Under the Interstate Highway Act of 1956 more than thirty-thousand miles of high-speed, limited access, cross-country freeways were constructed in little more than a decade. There were, then, good reasons why the American iron and steel industry, as did the American automotive industry, set their sights on the American market. But European and Japanese manufacturers were also attracted to the American market.

For the most part, the quarter-century between the close of World War II and 1970 were years of sustained growth and change. Indeed, Americans had difficulty adjusting to the rapid changes occurring. The growth of ever-larger corporate America, and the new, rapid, urban lifestyle, shifting populations, racial conflicts, and changing technology contributed to a rising disaffection among the young and some older Americans. American lifestyles were changed by antibiotics, polio vaccines, plastics, television, jet propulsion, the 45 rpm record, and American astronauts walking on the moon. Economic problems existed before 1970, but other than the problems of coping with relative abundance, they were not severe. However, underlying economic problems, characterized by rising competition from Europe and Japan, and focusing largely on the automotive, steel, and petroleum industries, became pervasive in the next quarter-century.

As a result of these domestic transformations, America's global economic hegemony disintegrated rapidly in the decades after 1970. The 1970s, particularly, was a decade of crisis. An OPEC petroleum embargo, the demise of the "gold" dollar as the world's benchmark currency, the Vietnam War, and the concession of the Panama Canal were all indicative of a rapidly changing world order. But there were other subliminal changes occurring in that first quarter-century that would place the United States on a different footing in the world than it had ever been before. Although the United States would no longer be the dominant economic world power, there were new elements of the American business system that would permeate the changing global economy. Computers and communications, aerospace and aeronautics, soft drinks and fast foods coupled with the dynamic agribusiness sector and a rejuvenated automobile and steel industry combined to create a new American global economic presence. That new presence, although not dominant, was nonetheless pervasive. It grew out of the peculiar global conditions associated with Cold War commerce.

Chapter 5

COLD WAR COMMERCE

Until the latest of our world conflicts, the United States had no armaments industry. American makers of plowshares could, with time and as required, make swords as well.

But we can no longer risk emergency improvisation of national defense. We have been compelled to create a permanent armaments industry of vast proportions. Added to this, three and a half million men and women are directly engaged in the defense establishment. We annually spend on military security alone more than the net income of all United States corporations.

— Dwight D. Eisenhower, "Farewell Address," January 17, 1961

As after previous wars, American defense industries following World War II rapidly converted from manufacturing swords into the manufacture of plowshares. U.S. defense spending dropped from its 1945 high of $98.3 billion to one-third that ($32.9 billion) by 1948. But in that year the Soviet Union blocked American and Allied entry to occupied sectors of Berlin. President Truman responded with a Berlin Airlift. American cargo planes (C-54s for the most part) carried food, fuel, and supplies to the Western-occupied city of Berlin. In April 1949, the North Atlantic Treaty Organization (NATO) came into being, creating a mutual defense pact among the United States, Great Britain, France, Italy, Belgium, the Netherlands, Luxembourg, Denmark, Norway, Portugal, Iceland, and Canada (joined later by Greece,

Dwight D. Eisenhower
(from the collections of The Library of Congress)

Turkey, and West Germany). Those nations agreed that an attack against any one of them would be considered an attack against all.

In September 1949, the Soviet Union exploded an atomic bomb, undermining America's "nuclear shield." That same year, Mao Tse-tung's communist armies succeeded in driving the nationalist armies of General Chiang Kai-shek from the mainland into Formosa (Taiwan). In 1950, North Korean armies from the Soviet-occupied sector north of the 38th parallel struck South Korea. The United Nations condemned the attack, and UN forces (comprising 90 percent American units) under General Douglas MacArthur rushed to the defense of South Korea. The Korean War affirmed an American commitment to a permanent defense industry. Defense and the Cold War dominated global affairs for the next three decades.

The Cold War divided the world into two hemispheres: an East and West, a Soviet-Chinese and an American-dominated sphere. Defense expenditures comprised a large portion of expenditures of nations within both sectors. From 1950 through 1970 one-half of the expenditures of the U.S. government were for defense. Although most armament sales by American manufacturers were to the U.S. government, private industry sold additional billions of dollars worth of armaments abroad. Agricultural production and marketing, energy industries (prominently petroleum), and most civilian sectors of the U.S. economy were greatly shaped and influenced by the Cold War. The Cold War was the overriding condition affecting American business and commerce and the world economic community after World War II.

THE WORLD'S BUSINESS: DEFENSE

The commerce of the Cold War had much to do with supplying the armies of the United States and Western nations with the ships, aircraft, bombs, tanks, missiles, small arms, munitions, and equipment believed necessary to defend NATO members or later, Southeast Asia Treaty Organization (SEATO) members against attack by the Soviet Union and its allies. Until 1960 almost all of that military equipment came from American corporations.

Following the Berlin blockade, the United States and NATO expected an attack at any time in Europe. Congress escalated defense spending with an initial appropriation in 1950 of $1.5 billion to help arm NATO forces in Europe. In 1951 the president recalled General Dwight D. Eisenhower from active duty to head NATO armies. Defense spending rose to $44 billion that year and jumped to $65 billion the year following. Throughout the 1950s almost one-half of total federal spending was for defense. Defense spending rose steadily through the Korean War (1948–1952), stabilized somewhat between 1953 and 1957, and then rose sharply from 1958 through 1964. The U.S. government actively encouraged the development of a private arms industry, closely associated with the defense establishment, which excelled in the design and production of high-technology weapons. Concurrently, as described by Jacob Goodwin, author of *Brotherhood of Arms: General Dynamics and the Business of Defending America,* scientists, technicians, and academics looked to Washington, especially to the Department of Defense, for financial support. Many corporations, cities, and regions in America became dependent upon employment and profits derived from weapons manufacture.

The Korean War and U.S./NATO defense policies also stimulated the development of a permanent arms industry abroad. U.S. military grants and orders for arms resulted in the reconstruction of United Kingdom, French, and West German armament industries. In a dozen years between 1949 and 1962, the U.S. government sold on its own account $16.1 billion worth of armaments abroad and gave to allied or associated nations another $30.2 billion in armaments. By 1976, U.S. grants to its allies for military preparedness totaled $69 billion. The United States actively encouraged the restoration and development of arms manufacturing by its NATO allies. Through somewhat complex and often highly political procurement arrangements, NATO nations increasingly began to share Western armament markets.

NATO managed its resources through twenty advisory committees. The Economic Committee, the Senior NATO Logistics Conference, and the NATO Standardization Group were primarily concerned with NATO procurement policies. Other offices included the Advisory Group for Aerospace Research and Development, the Military Agency for Standardization, and an Electronic Advisory Committee. NATO agencies with procurement responsibilities included the Maintenance and Supply Agency, headquartered in Luxembourg, which provided logistics support for selected weapons systems. The European Fighter Aircraft Development Production and Logistics Management Agency located in Unterhacking, Germany, monitored the development, production, and logistics of NATO European fighter aircraft. The Central Europe Operating Agency managed the Central Europe Pipeline System from offices in Versailles, France. The Hawk Management Office located in Rueil-Malmaison, France, directed procurement of the Hawk surface-to-air missile system. Numerous other agencies directed specific procurement tasks. Cold War defense procurement stimulated production and technological development within the United States and abroad.

French manufacturers, stimulated by American purchases and grants, stressed the production of heavy cannon, artillery, mortars, bazookas, and machine guns and began the development of what would become the highly successful Mirage fighter aircraft. British Centurion tanks and the Patton-class M-47 and M-48 tanks (manufactured by Chrysler Corporation) became the mainstay of European battle forces. Chrysler began development of what would eventually become the M-1 Abrams tank in 1963. During the 1960s the U.S. Navy converted from its historic procurement practice—that is, building their own ships in government shipyards—to contract procurement with private industry. Electric Boat (a division of General Dynamics), Newport News, and Ingalls dominated naval ship production. In 1968 the federal government planned to spend $1.6 billion for the construction and modification of naval vessels. The budget included $8.9 billion for new aircraft and another $1.1 billion for development of a new generation of "swing-wing" planes. Lockheed Aircraft was to receive $500 million for production of C-5A cargo transport airplanes; Ling-Temco-Vought was under contract for $670 million of the A-5 attack aircraft, whereas McDonnell Douglas was to build $576 million worth of F-4 supersonic fighters.

Although in the beginning of the Cold War the United States dominated arms manufacture and sales among Western nations, in the 1960s the United Kingdom, France, Belgium, and the Netherlands accounted for an increasing part of Western armaments. The rejuvenation of French arms manufactures contributed to a 1966 decision by France to withdraw from NATO forces. Subsequently, France became increasingly active in international arms markets and increasingly competitive with American arms manufacturers selling in the global market.

According to a Brookings Institute study, between 1966 and 1970 the United States supplied $13.4 billion worth of armaments in the world markets, the Soviet Union $7.7 billion, France $900 million, and China $830 million, followed closely by the United Kingdom, West Germany, Czechoslovakia, Canada, Poland, and other nations.

In 1962, the United States spent $106 billion on defense, and by the close of the decade defense spending approached $200 billion a year. (In the 1960s the proportion of the federal budget allocated to defense actually declined, despite rapid increases in total spending, because of great increases in government spending for social programs.) Most defense dollars went for aircraft, nuclear submarines, Forrestal-class aircraft carriers, tanks (such as the new Patton tank), nuclear weapons, missiles, radar and sonar equipment, computers and research, and development of the technology of modern warfare.

Whereas World War II guns and tanks and aircraft bore a strong resemblance to the guns, vehicles, and airplanes used in the civilian economy and often could be readily adapted to civilian uses and civilian markets, as time passed, military hardware bore less resemblance to civilian equipment. Hypersonic aircraft had no civilian counterpart; missiles and nuclear weapons could not be converted to civilian uses. Weapons became increasingly sophisticated, and the constant pressure to develop new weapons technology grew greater and more costly. Research and development costs became a much larger portion of defense expenditures. Nations, including the United States, bought armaments based on their performance, not on their costs.

Defense expenditures increasingly supplemented the research and development costs of private manufacturers. Corporations were reluctant to use private capital for pure research or development. Pure research resulted in deferred or even nonexistent profits. Civilian production emphasized costs and profits, not performance. The "American System of Manufacturing" long stressed the production of a "good" product at a "good" price, not a high-quality or "finished" product at a high price. Military procurement on the other hand, whether a rifle, aircraft, or missile, demanded high performance, accuracy, and reliability. Defense production required, even more than under the European tradition of refined manufacture, intensive research, development, testing and refinement, and correspondingly greater costs per unit manufactured.

As time passed, defense industries became increasingly unlike their private-sector counterparts and increasingly dependent upon government "cost-plus" contracts. Manufacturers of goods and services for the civilian market historically invested in market studies and market development rather than in pure research. American business also traditionally invested in "refinement," or product development, for the civilian market. The problem was that products "researched and developed" for defense purposes often held no immediate relevance to the civilian marketplace. New technology developed from defense research and development (R&D) did not easily transfer to the civilian sector. The necessity for secrecy or confidentiality in high-tech military procurement delayed or stymied technology transfer to civilian industries. Moreover, American firms were hesitant to invest capital in new technology when expansion of existing production seemed to generate immediate profits. Stockholders and management desired early, not delayed, profits. Given the great investment made by the taxpayer in military research and development, technology transfer to the private sector became a growing concern.

Because of the stress on performance and new technology, and the high costs associated with defense products, the defense sector of the private economy became apprenticed to government. Defense contractors tended to become adjuncts of the Department of Defense. Corporations that produced armaments became increasingly

TABLE 5–1
Federal Government Defense Expenditures, 1950–1970

Year	Total Spending in Billions	Total Defense Outlays in Billions	Defense Percent Total
1950	$39.5	$13.5	34%
1951	43.9	20.8	47%
1952	65.3	40.6	62%
1953	74.1	44.0	59%
1954	70.1	40.6	58%
1955	68.5	35.6	52%
1956	70.5	35.7	51%
1957	76.7	38.7	50%
1958	82.6	40.1	49%
1959	92.1	44.6	48%
1960	92.2	43.9	48%
1961	97.8	45.7	47%
1962	106.8	49.2	46%
1963	111.3	49.2	44%
1964	118.6	50.7	43%
1965	118.4	47.2	40%
1966	134.6	55.4	41%
1967	158.3	68.8	43%
1968	178.8	78.7	44%
1969	184.6	79.1	43%
1970	196.6	78.4	40%

Source: Historical Statistics of the United States Colonial Times to 1970, Series F 1-5 and Y 457–65, 224, 1114.

specialized, and often they became less diversified and more concentrated in their defense production. For example, defense contracts accounted for 88 percent of Lockheed Aircraft's sales from 1961 to 1967 and 75 percent of McDonnell Douglas sales. General Dynamics, which often led the list of corporations receiving the largest dollar volume of defense contracts, did 67 percent of its business with the Department of Defense. General Dynamic's Convair Division manufactured the Atlas missile, several Navy missiles, the F-102 and F-106 hypersonic fighters, and components of the new B-58 bomber. Boeing Aircraft continued to manufacture the stalwart B-52 bomber for several decades after the end of World War II. In 1958, following the Soviet Union's Sputnik spectacular in 1957, Boeing's defense contracts more than doubled from $907 million to $2.1 billion. Meanwhile, North American Aviation's work focused heavily on research and development. It developed the Vigilante attack plane, the T-39 Sabre jet, the B-70, the X-15 experimental aircraft, and the Hound Dog air-to-surface missile. North American also developed the guidance systems for Minuteman and Polaris missiles.

In 1968 the leading five defense contractors included General Dynamics, Lockheed Aircraft, General Electric, United Aircraft, and McDonnell Douglas. General Dynamics had contracts exceeding $2.2 billion that ranged from the alteration, repair, and maintenance of naval vessels to the development and production of the new F-111 fighter aircraft. Lockheed Aircraft, the second most important defense manufacturer, produced the C-5A Galaxy Jet Transport, the C-141A Starlifter Jet Cargo Transport, the F-104 Starfighter, the P-3 Orion Patrol Bomber, and the Cheyenne helicopter. Lockheed was also the primary contractor for the Navy's Polaris and Poseidon missiles. United Aircraft, with $1.3 billion under Department of Defense contract, manufactured the large CH-54 Flying Crane, SH-3D Sea King, and CH-53 Sea Stallion helicopters. McDonnell Douglas Corporation produced the F-4 Phantom series fighter and reconnaissance aircraft, the A-4/TA-4 Jet Attack/Trainer Aircraft, and was a major contractor for the Air Force Manned Orbiting Laboratory (later assumed by NASA as a part of the space station program).

In 1968, the top 100 corporations accounted for 67 percent of the nation's defense business. They employed hundreds of thousands of Americans—including, thought Senator William Proxmire (D–Wisc.), too many retired officers and civilian government officials. Critics and supporters both began talking about America's "military-industrial" complex.

THE MILITARY-INDUSTRIAL COMPLEX

Proxmire, the Senate's inveterate spending conscience, identified a "community of interests" between the military and defense contractors in his 1970 *Report from the Wasteland: America's Military-Industrial Complex.* Proxmire compared the number of high-ranking retired military personnel working for defense contractors in 1969 with those so employed in 1959: Three times the number were employed in 1969. Proxmire warned against the danger of having military contracts let by military officers to corporations run by former military officers. It precluded, he thought, critical review, fostered waste, and promoted "tunnel vision" in defense spending.

Just as Proxmire decried the omnipresence of retired military and civilian government employees among corporate administrators in the defense industries, others, including Seymour Melman (a professor of industrial engineering at Columbia University and author of *Pentagon Capitalism* and other books with a related theme) attached a sinister significance to the apparent dominance of defense in research and development in the United States. Melman estimated in 1963 that two-thirds to three-fourths of all engineers and scientists in the country worked directly or indirectly for the Department of Defense. He believed that defense spending siphoned resources from civilian industries, resulted in the neglect of social problems, and slowed the rate of economic growth.

Notwithstanding the community of interests, which undoubtedly existed, and the collusion that may have occurred, the significance of Proxmire's and Seymour's data is that virtually all of the American dollars spent on defense went to American corporations, American engineers, and American labor. Indeed, many of the francs and pounds spent by NATO allies were for the purchase of American armaments. The defense industry dominated Cold War commerce and greatly influenced developing transportation and communications industries on a global scale.

The 100 largest corporations in 1968, ranked by the value of their prime military contracts, are indicated in Table 5-2 on pages 80-81. Many of these corporations and prominently those in aerospace such as General Dynamics, Lockheed Aircraft, McDonnell Douglas, Boeing Corporation, and North American Rockwell Corporation also held large NASA contracts. Most cooperated with each other on procurement contracts through subcontracting. Thousands of small businesses participated as defense suppliers through subcontracts with the larger primary contractor. Although the bulk of defense spending went to a relatively small number of large corporations, the monies tended to be dispersed throughout the civilian economy through subcontracting arrangements by virtue of the geographically dispersed defense facilities and, of course, through employee payrolls and stockholders dividends.

The Armed Service Procurement Act of 1947 removed some of the contract and procurement restrictions that usually applied in peacetime. The Act enabled the government to avoid competitive bidding under certain circumstances, to deal with single suppliers, and to abbreviate the contract negotiation process. The result was to speed production, but also, many argue, to encourage waste, inefficiencies, error, and the development of a virtual partnership between industry and government. Defense contracts were usually cost-plus-fixed-fee contracts, essentially eliminating the marketplace from the award.

Throughout the Cold War, defense spending accounted for approximately 10 percent of the total civilian economy. About 10 percent of the labor force was employed in military-related industry. Did defense spending produce or retard long-term economic growth? The answers are still inconclusive. Although it may be difficult to assess the net results of defense spending, it made direct and often positive impacts on economic growth and development. A clear impetus for the Interstate Highway Act of 1954 came from the necessity for rapid East-West military transit and the precedent of the German autobahn. Even though it is a civilian agency (at the instigation of President Dwight D. Eisenhower), NASA had strong defense ramifications. Spinoffs from defense technology created the nuclear energy industry and strongly influenced developments in metallurgy, electronics, robotics, communications, transportation, and medicine. Videocassette cameras and videotape recorders, infrared cameras, laptop computers, and the computer Internet system resulted from military procurement. More broadly, federal programs, often associated with defense spending such as the GI Bill, guaranteed student loan programs, grants, and research and development contracts with universities helped in the creation and dispersion of new science and technology.

Some aspects of defense spending went beyond market or even military considerations. Military spending also had to do with American foreign policy. Military contracts and NASA contracts, coupled with Marshall Plan spending and other foreign aid programs, combined to provide the substance of American foreign policy during the Cold War. Defense contracts, NATO procurement policies, and grants to foreign nations for the purchase of armaments often had as much to do with diplomacy as with defense. But in the final analysis, defense and diplomacy rested upon the strength of the American economy.

As General Omar Bradley advised Congress in 1949, when the United States began to contemplate the emerging realities of the Cold War, "a nation's economy is its ultimate strength." Similarly, Gabriel Kolko stressed in his important study of *The Roots of American Foreign Policy* that the real interests and purposes of American foreign policy are *"not to fight wars but to gain vital strategic and economic objectives that materially enlarge American power everywhere."* Thus, a fundamental significance of military contracting goes beyond the actual armament manufactured or placed into service and lies in the enhancement of American manufacturing capability and in developing the economy's overall strength.

During the first few decades following World War II, the American military presence and American-produced armaments had a relatively stronger influence on the world than did American civilian manufactures. In those early years of the Cold War, Europe and Asia had little money for the purchase of American consumer goods. The world bought American armaments for defense, American machine tools, plants, and equipment to rebuild shattered economies, and American farm products to satisfy the critical production shortfalls in their own countries. The source of American power had to do with defense spending and economic reconstruction as much as it did with the reality of sheer military power and armaments.

To be sure, commerce during the Cold War involved more than armaments. The United States exported arms and armies, machine tools, and food and fiber. Americans imported fuel, automobiles, and consumer goods. Despite the massive production of domestic manufacturers, the products of American industry could not alone meet the demands of the U.S. market. For most of the first two decades following World War II, the United States consumed most of the world's exported goods and services.

American imports rose rapidly after 1954 as European and Asian industries were rebuilt and production resumed. Japan experienced a phenomenal rate of growth in its Gross Domestic Product (GDP) between 1960 and 1970, with a 150 percent increase. Much of that growth was accounted for by American purchases of Japanese automobiles and Japanese electronics. West Germany, France, the United Kingdom, and Italy each exceeded the United States in the decade of the 1960s in their growth in productivity. Americans purchased automobiles, fuel, shoes, electronics, toys, food and alcoholic beverages, and travel from Europe. For example, American expenditures for foreign travel (most of that to European destinations) shot up from $831 million in 1951 to $4.8 billion in 1970.

Japanese and European economic recovery contributed to declining U.S. exports of basic agricultural commodities, iron, steel, machinery, and equipment. Europe and Asian manufacturers focused more on producing the consumer goods demanded by the seemingly insatiable American consumer. Moreover, they produced those goods

TABLE 5–2

The 100 Largest Corporations
Ranked by Prime Military Contracts in 1968

INDEX OF 100 PARENT COMPANIES WHICH,
WITH THEIR SUBSIDIARIES, RECEIVED THE LARGEST
DOLLAR VOLUME OF MILITARY PRIME CONTRACT AWARDS IN FY 1968

Rank Parent Company	Rank Parent Company
89. Aerodex, Inc.	56. Fairchild Hiller Corp.
74. Aerospace Corp. (N)	82. Federal Cartridge Corp.
61. American Machine & Foundry Co.	19. Ford Motor Co.
71. American Mfg. Co. of Texas	1. General Dynamics Corp.
6. American Telephone & Telegraph Co.	3. General Electric Co.
	10. General Motors Corp.
49. Asiatic Petroleum Corp.	63. General Precision Equipment Corp.
94. Atlas Chemical Industries, Inc.	41. General Telephone & Electronics Corp.
99. Automatic Sprinkler Corp. of America	
12. A V C O Corp.	28. General Tire & Rubber Co.
31. Bendix Corp.	48. Goodyear Tire & Rubber Co.
7. Boeing Co.	11. Grumman Aircraft Engineering Corp.
75. Cessna Aircraft Co.	78. Gulf Oil Corp.
62. Chamberlain Corp.	96. Harris-Intertype Corp.
43. Chrysler Corp.	65. Harvey Aluminum, Inc.
68. City Investing Co.	93. Hazeltine Corp.
47. Collins Radio Co.	37. Hercules, Inc.
69. Colt Industries, Inc.	20. Honeywell, Inc.
79. Condec Corp.	24. Hughes Aircraft Co.
81. Continental Air Lines, Inc.	83. Hughes Tool Co.
86. Control Data Corp.	30. International Business Machines Co.
72. Curtiss Wright Corp.	
40. Day & Zimmerman, Inc.	98. International Harvester Co.
38. DuPont E. I. De Nemour & Co.	29. International Telephone & Tel. Corp.
59. Eastman Kodak Co.	
76. Emerson Electric Co.	85. Johns Hopkins University (N)
33. F M C Corp.	18. Kaiser Industries Corp.

*Raymond International, Inc.; Morrison-Knudsen Co., Inc.; Brown & Root, Inc.; & J. A. Jones Construction Co.

(N) Nonprofit

(JV) Joint Venture

Source: Seymour Melman, *The Defense Economy* (New York: Praeger Publishers, 1970), 400.

TABLE 5–2 (CONTINUED)
The 100 Largest Corporations
Ranked by Prime Military Contracts in 1968

**INDEX OF 100 PARENT COMPANIES WHICH,
WITH THEIR SUBSIDIARIES, RECEIVED THE LARGEST
DOLLAR VOLUME OF MILITARY PRIME CONTRACT AWARDS IN FY 1968**

Rank	Parent Company	Rank	Parent Company
64.	Lear Siegler, Inc.	35.	Raymond Morrison Knudsen (JV)*
8.	Ling Temco Vought, Inc.	15.	Raytheon Co.
14.	Litton Industries, Inc.	23.	Ryan Aeronautical Co.
2.	Lockheed Aircraft Corp.	50.	Sanders Associates, Inc.
87.	Lykes Corp.	77.	Seatrain Lines, Inc.
55.	Magnavox Co.	36.	Signal Companies, Inc. (The)
17.	Martin Marietta Corp.	100.	Smith Investment Co.
53.	Mason & Hanger Silas Mason Co.	16.	Sperry Rand Corp.
54.	Massachusetts Institute of Technology	44.	Standard Oil Co. of Calif.
		25.	Standard Oil of New Jersey
5.	McDonnell Douglas Corp.	92.	States Marine Lines, Inc.
88.	McLean Industries, Inc.	90.	Susquehanna Corp.
51.	Mobil Oil Corp.	91.	Sverdrup & Parcel & Associates, Inc.
80.	Motorola, Inc.	52.	T R W, Inc.
66.	National Presto Industries, Inc.	67.	Teledyne, Inc.
34.	Newport News Shipbuilding & Dry Dock Co.	46.	Texaco, Inc.
		39.	Texas Instruments, Inc.
45.	Norris Industries	13.	Textron, Inc.
9.	North American Rockwell Corp.	58.	Thiokol Chemical Corp.
		42.	Uniroyal, Inc.
22.	Northrop Corp.	4.	United Aircraft Corp.
21.	Olin Mathieson Chemical Corp.	60.	United States Steel Corp.
		95.	Vinnell Corp.
57.	Pacific Architects & Engineers, Inc.	84.	Vitro Corp. of America
		70.	Western Union Telegraph Co.
32.	Pan American World Airways, Inc.	27.	Westinghouse Electric Corp.
		73.	White Motor Co.
26.	Radio Corp. of America	97.	World Airways, Inc.

with new and improved plants and equipment and paid much less than comparable labor in the United States.

Despite two decades of remarkable economic growth the American trade balance turned negative in 1971 for the first time since 1893. The trade imbalance continued to grow while the United States devolved from its position as the world's premier economic

*President of Occidental Petroleum Corporation of Los Angeles, Armand
Hammer (left), had a strong commitment to global commerce. Here he
meets with Soviet leader Nikita Khrushchev at the Kremlin in Moscow on
March 14, 1961.*

(Reuters/Bettmann Newsphotos)

and military power to becoming, while still the major power, one
among a number of growing federated global economies. Hesitantly,
but with growing assurance, the United States turned from producing goods for the domestic market to producing and marketing goods
and services for the global economy. Among the pioneers in taking
American business abroad was the remarkable Armand Hammer.

TAKING AMERICA'S BUSINESS ABROAD: ARMAND HAMMER

A controversial and enterprising global merchant who defied the
seemingly rigid boundaries defined by the Cold War, but who never-

theless helped awaken Americans to the global marketplace, was Armand Hammer. Named for the Soviet symbol "arm and hammer" by his father Julius, a physician, socialist, and New York–born son of Russian emigres, Armand Hammer began selling pharmaceuticals and then grain to revolutionary Russia in the 1920s.

In 1921 he applied for a passport for travel to Russia, in part to collect $150,000 owed his family's Allied Drug and Chemical Corporation by the Bolshevik government, and in part to see the birthplace of his parents and grandparents. To smooth the way for his travels in Russia, Hammer sent a fully equipped field hospital to the Russian government in advance of his arrival. Despite reservations by the Federal Bureau of Investigation (and J. Edgar Hoover in particular) and official concern about the propriety of dealing with the communist revolutionary government, Hammer received his passport.

Upon his arrival in Russia and during travels through the countryside, he encountered widespread mass starvation. He realized then that there was something he could do for the Russian people and something for himself. Invited to meet personally with Vladimir I. Lenin, Hammer negotiated an agreement by which Hammer received a concession to sell grain to the Soviet Union, in exchange for payment in furs, lumber, semiprecious stones, and for asbestos mining rights. Lenin believed it important to establish links with Western and American capitalists in order to diminish Western hostility and to encourage recognition of the revolutionary government by Western nations.

Nevertheless, since tensions remained high between the United States and the Soviet Union through the 1920s and 1930s, Armand Hammer's business relations with the communist government gave him a degree of notoriety. But he sought more than profit. Hammer believed that his trade associations were "helping a struggling nation achieve self-sufficiency, aiding the American government's balance of trade, and making a contribution to international understanding." To do all of that and to make a profit were in the best traditions of American capitalism.

After World War II, the fall of the Iron Curtain and the Cold War replicated to an extent those conditions existing between the United States and the Soviet Union in the 1920s and 1930s. Armand Hammer reestablished both his notoriety and his usefulness to the American government by becoming a "Cold War capitalist" with Soviet connections. Instead of pharmaceuticals and grain, he now sought oil and offered agricultural chemicals.

His vehicle for trade was to be Occidental Petroleum Corporation. Hammer invested in the Los Angeles–based oil exploration company in 1956, fully expecting to lose money and take his losses as a tax write-off. Instead, Occidental struck oil. Hammer made money—in enormous quantities. Occidental became, under his supervision, a highly successful, but (compared to Exxon, Texaco, Mobil, and others) small petroleum exploration and producing company. Occidental, however, developed global enterprises rivaling those of the largest U.S. companies.

Hammer met Soviet Premier Nikita Khrushchev at a dinner given by Eleanor Roosevelt at Hyde Park in September 1959. In 1961, with the blessings of President John F. Kennedy and with the logistical support of the Department of Commerce, Hammer and his wife, Frances, left for a visit to the Soviet Union. During his travels Hammer found the world peculiarly bereft of an American commercial presence.

In Italy, he was perplexed by the absence of American appliances in the stores. He discovered, for example, that American refrigerators, although generally superior to Italian products and often priced lower, were not bought in Italy simply because they were physically too large for the typical Italian household. When he inquired about the revolutionary IBM mainframe computers that had already become essentials in the American business world, he discovered that only twenty-eight computers were in Italy, and there were half that number of qualified operators to use them. On a stopover in Libya, then a North African nation with seemingly little economic consequence, Hammer found an oil rush in progress. He counted nineteen Western oil companies doing business there and an equal number hoping to obtain concessions. But many of the agreements entered into, he thought, were of questionable value. Western companies and the American government had little experience with doing business in Libya. Neither did Hammer, but he did know something about doing business abroad, and he knew that Western companies were making many critical mistakes. Hammer wrote Luther Hodges, President Kennedy's secretary of commerce, urging that the American government assist in the development of closer commercial ties with Italy. Hammer looked forward to taking Occidental into Libya. He traveled on to the Soviet Union.

His business in Moscow produced remarkable results considering the extreme tensions between the United States and the Soviet Union. Hammer met first with a number of Russian trade officials, then with Anastas Mikoyan, the first deputy premier. They reviewed a few of the critical conflicts between the former allies: the Soviet Union's failure to settle lend-lease debts, Vice President Richard Nixon's hostile comments during a 1959 visit to Moscow, the American ban on importing Soviet crab meat, and the need for direct commercial air service between the Soviet Union and the United States. Much to the surprise and in some cases the chagrin of American embassy officials in Moscow, who had considered Hammer as a 1920s anachronism rather than a modern global businessman, he received an invitation to visit with Premier Nikita Khrushchev. Upon his return to the United States and following visits with American State Department officials and reports to Eleanor Roosevelt (and to the American press), Hammer's advice on American-Soviet affairs was frequently sought by President Kennedy and his successor, Lyndon B. Johnson. Hammer became an accepted, important, and even celebrated unofficial link to the Soviet Union. Business became an important element in establishing detente with the Soviet Union and in reducing the tensions of the Cold War.

Meanwhile, the discovery of a major gas field in California catapulted Occidental's bottom line from a $170 loss in 1960 to a $7 million profit in 1963. Occidental kept growing at home and abroad. Hammer capitalized on Occidental gas discoveries by branching out into agricultural chemicals. Major acquisitions of sulphur, phosphate, and nitrogen manufactures enabled him to enter foreign petroleum markets with a simple but effective offer. Occidental offered fertilizers in exchange for oil. In the 1960s Hammer began negotiations to develop fertilizer plants in Saudi Arabia, Nicaragua, Venezuela, Singapore, Turkey, Morocco, Tunisia, and Libya. He obtained the long-sought oil drilling rights for Occidental in Libya, and in the United States he continued to add oil, gas, and coal companies and reserves.

To be sure, Hammer was a Johnny-come-lately to Mideast oil. Standard Oil, Gulf, and Texaco began oil exploration in Saudi Arabia and the Arab Emirates in the 1920s. The ARAMCO Oil consortium was formed in 1933, and after World War II the United States became increasingly dependent upon imported oil from the Middle East. The fascinating thing about Hammer is in part that he presumed to tackle the entrenched interests of "big oil," and did so successfully. Hammer reflected a new, independent entrepreneurial spirit that in the 1960s was beginning to create a new American presence in the global marketplace. Other than for oil, through the 1960s, the United

States had been in the position of being buyers rather than sellers. The United States sold abroad, but those sales occurred for the most part because the United States was the sole supplier. By the 1960s American products began to encounter growing competition from foreign producers. IBM, for example, pressed its international expansion during the decade of the 1960s, after European and Asian companies had already developed competing products.

IBM AND WORLD TRADE

In 1949, foreign sales (other than Canada) accounted for $6.3 million or 5 percent of IBM's net revenues of $119 million. In that year IBM organized its World Trade Corporation to handle overseas sales. IBM's CEO, Tom Watson, turned the management of World Trade over to his son, Dick Watson, who organized the first of IBM's overseas affiliates, IBM United Kingdom. IBM United Kingdom offered shares to U.K. investors. Its overseas offices were to be managed by U.K. managers. IBM received the rights to produce and market IBM products in the United Kingdom. Overseas plants and equipment were turned over by IBM to its overseas affiliates, which in turn reported to IBM World Trade. Other American companies, such as RCA and General Electric, generally pursued licensing agreements with companies in other nations rather than setting up independent affiliates. RCA, for example, entered the Japanese market by licensing its patents to Hitachi; Honeywell associated with Nippon Electric; TRW and Westinghouse worked with Mitsubishi Electric; and Sperry Rand collaborated with Oki Denki. As American corporations began to establish a presence in overseas economies, even those of friendly, allied, or NATO nations, those countries inevitably began to build up deterrents to American trade in order to protect their own recovering or developing industry.

Thus Japan sought to counter IBM Japan by creating a giant computer marketing and production consortium of its six largest electronic firms, including Nippon Electric, Hitachi, Fujitsu, Toshiba, Oki Denki, and Mitsubishi. These firms created their own computer giant, the Japan Electronic Computer Company Ltd., supported by government financial assistance and marketing opportunities. Despite the organized resistance in Japan, IBM Japan succeeded in winning about 30 percent of the market for computer equipment. In Great Britain, IBM overcame fierce competition to lead British firms in computer sales (and leases) by the close of the decade of the 1960s. IBM became increasingly global during the 1960s as the domestic markets reached saturation. Between 1949 and 1969, IBM's earnings from its international business rose from 5 percent to more than one-third of domestic earnings.

The computer market in the 1960s was for the large IBM 1400 and 7000-type computers. In addition, IBM and its international competitors generally leased rather than sold these machines. But, computer technology was rapidly changing from the electronic tube to the transistor to the integrated circuit composition. The nature of the computer industry changed drastically within a short time and IBM was reluctant to change with the times.

Texas Instruments' Gordon Teal developed the silicone transistor in 1954. An integrated circuit by TI's Jack Kilby received considerable momentum by virtue of its use in Apollo guidance systems and in the Minuteman missile, demonstrating the pervasive influence of defense technology on civilian markets. Texas Instruments pioneered in integrated circuits, and by the mid-1960s IBM and other electronic data manufacturers were converting to the new systems. As discussed in following chapters, the character of the computer industry changed markedly—and so did the computer marketplace.

Indeed, the whole structure and character of world markets began to change rapidly in the 1960s as European and Asian manufacturers came "online." Dependency on the American corporation declined in almost every product line, from defense to consumer goods to energy. Relatively, American sales abroad of computers, aircraft, tanks, ammunition, and automobiles declined, whereas American purchases of products from abroad continued to rise. For the most part, the process was slow, and the American business response to international competition did not obtain momentum for another decade. Meanwhile, a crisis in the petroleum industry in the early 1970s focused American attention on the changing global market as nothing else could.

Near the end of the decade of the 1960s, Occidental and Hammer had become involved in explorations and political intrigue in the Mideast that brought the oil-rich sheikdom of Umm al Qaiwan, Libya, Iran, Saudi Arabia, Great Britain, and the United States, if not the entire world, to a critical juncture. By the close of the decade of the 1960s, Occidental and American petroleum companies in the Middle East faced confiscation and the nationalization of their holdings. The United States and the world faced a revolutionary change in the way petroleum would be marketed and most notably in the price at which it would be marketed. During the 1960s America's position within the global community was altered.

American business lost its competitive edge. The American economy developed a trade imbalance and the United States became a major but no longer a dominant factor in the global economy. The economy and the society experienced convulsions. Young Americans began to reject the Cold War and the obligation of military service that it entailed. The United States abolished the draft and opted for a more costly but perhaps more efficient volunteer army. Some younger Americans rejected what they regarded as the sordid materialism of the postwar American capitalist society and entered a form of hedonistic withdrawal from the world. Other Americans protested that they were deprived entry to that same materialistic culture being rejected by "hippies." Affluence seemed reserved only for white, Anglo-Saxon, protestant Americans (WASPs). Minorities, particularly African Americans, demanded and painstakingly obtained more equal economic and political opportunities and, in some if not many instances, improved their material welfare and obtained a better quality of life. Although the 1960s had been a socially uneasy and difficult time domestically, the following decade brought new international crises and desperate times for defense, finance, and business abroad. The post–World War II American economic and military hegemony was coming to a close.

Part 2
—

THE GLOBALIZATION OF
THE AMERICAN ECONOMY
1970–1995

Chapter 6

THE CHANGING WORLD ORDER

Despite twenty-five years of remarkable economic growth, the United States after 1970 began to devolve as the world's premier economic and military power. While it would continue to produce the single largest part of the world's gross product and to consume a proportionately greater share of that product, the United States no longer retained its position of economic hegemony. A decade of crises forced a realignment of American relations with the global community and began the process of redirecting American business from its historic preoccupation with the American market to a larger global awareness. Hesitantly, but with growing assurance, American businesses turned from producing goods for the domestic market to producing and marketing goods and services for the global market.

The troubles encountered by the United States in the 1970s were many. In 1971 the American trade balance turned negative for the first time since 1893. Earlier, as a premonition of growing economic duress, the United States abandoned its historic support of gold at $35 per ounce and soon abandoned all efforts to maintain a fixed price for gold. Inflation was followed by experiments in wage and price controls. A sudden OPEC embargo on petroleum in 1973 created new financial crises in the United States and other Western nations. Concurrently, U.S. trading partners, including Europe and Japan, seemed to become more competitive and threatening to U.S. interests. Economic problems, coupled with military failures in Vietnam, cost the United States credibility at home and abroad. The

Soviet bloc, or as President Ronald Reagan would later identify it, "the Evil Empire," seemed ever more menacing.

THE DEMISE OF THE DOLLAR

The first premonition that something was wrong occurred in 1968, when Western trading nations, led by the United States, agreed to distinguish between the "official" price of gold and the "private market" price. Central banks could buy and sell gold at the official price of $35 per ounce. But in the "private" or unofficial market the price of gold floated free; that is, gold could sell at any price agreed to by a buyer and a seller. Speculators and countries with large balances of American dollars, such as France, were beginning to buy gold at higher than the U.S. guaranteed price of $35 per ounce anticipating that the United States would not be able to continue to redeem gold at that price. In other words, the value of the dollar was in doubt.

This monetary crisis, as it came to be, had some deep and complex roots. In international trade, gold was the historic medium of exchange or payment, but the physical exchange of gold coins or bullion is difficult and unwieldy. Rather, those engaging in the exchange of goods between nations became accustomed to accepting a particularly stable and strong national paper currency as the base for exchange. Those historically strong currencies, such as the British pound, became key *reserve currencies* because nations held those currencies for exchange purposes. Sales were usually made by quoting the price in reserve currency terms. Until World War II the British pound was the major reserve currency. After the war the American dollar became the dominant reserve currency. Foreign nations obtained American dollars through the regular processes of trade, but between 1945 and 1970 most of those dollars flowed into foreign treasuries as a result of American Marshall Plan aid, loans, defense expenditures, and capital investment.

By the late 1960s European nations in particular held large quantities of U.S. dollars, which represented demands on American gold held in the U.S. Treasury. The United States was obligated to accept those dollars in exchange for gold at the rate of $35 for each ounce of gold. It was doubtful that the United States had enough gold to cover its obligations. The market thus began to devalue the dollar. As devaluation occurred, the demands for gold at $35 per ounce rose. The U.S. response in 1968 to separate "official" demands for gold from "private" demands for gold would in theory reduce the pressures on gold and the dollar. This began the process of demonetizing gold and devaluing the dollar.

Underlying the growing pressure on the dollar were, among other things, rising defense costs caused by the growing involvement of U.S. forces in Vietnam. A South and North Vietnam came into being when France was forced to withdraw troops from the region. North Vietnam was under communist influence, and the United States attempted to sustain a republican government headed by President Ngo Dinh Diem in the South by sending aid and military advisers.

By 1961, when John F. Kennedy became president, the number of American military advisers had grown to 3200. When the Vietcong (the South Vietnamese guerrillas supportive of the North) and North Vietnamese regulars stepped up attacks on South Vietnam, the United States countered to the point that by 1968, under the direction of President Lyndon B. Johnson, the United States had more than half a million men in combat in South Vietnam. But the war went badly. Thousands of Americans were killed, captured, or missing in action. Costs escalated. Opposition within the United States rose. Finally, after the elections of 1968, newly elected President Richard M. Nixon promised to "wind down" the war in Vietnam. He attempted to do so by turning the war over to South Vietnamese forces while gradually withdrawing American forces. During the withdrawal the United States intensified its bombing runs over enemy territory, and the extraction of American forces proved prolonged and costly. In the end, Vietnam fell to enemy forces. The United States lost the war at the cost of 46,000 killed, 300,000 wounded, and more than $100 billion expended. Internationally, the United States lost both credibility and money. During the war in Vietnam, outlays for defense rose from about $50 billion annually to $80 billion.

During those war years, however, federal expenditures rose rapidly in areas *other* than defense, compounding the drain on the U.S. Treasury. John F. Kennedy's New Frontier advocated broad social reform and federal programs including broader Social Security coverage, extended public-housing assistance, federal aid for education, medical care for the aged, higher farm price supports, and more foreign aid, particularly for Latin America. But for Social Security and housing reforms, Congress failed to approve most of the New Frontier programs. Following the assassination of President Kennedy in 1963, Lyndon B. Johnson succeeded in obtaining passage of the Kennedy-Johnson agenda for a "Great Society."

Declaring "war on poverty," Johnson won legislation for mass transit in urban areas and for conservation of wilderness areas. The Elementary and Secondary Education Act of 1965 channeled new federal funds into public schools on the basis of the number of children from poor families in each school district. Another bill provided government rent subsidies to low-income families. Social Security benefits were raised, and Medicare became law. Federal expenditures rose sharply in space research and technology, health, Social Security, housing, education, and interest on the public debt. Government expenditures on public health soared from $1.7 billion in 1965 to almost $13 billion annually by 1970. Social Security costs increased by 60 percent to $44 billion annually. Federal expenditures for education increased fourfold, and community development and housing costs that had been practically nonexistent in 1965 became a $3 billion (and rising) cost five years later. Interest on the public debt also doubled. Between 1961 and 1970 federal expenditures more than doubled, from $97 to $196 billion annually, with most of the increase occurring after 1965.

Despite the massive rises in expenditures, federal spending as a proportion of GNP rose only slightly—testifying to the underlying strength and resilience of the economy. Nevertheless, domestic financial pressures on the United States mounted rapidly in the latter part of the 1960s during the Vietnam War. Contributing to those pressures was increased competition from America's own trading partners. Japan, West Germany, Great Britain, and France, and Europe generally, were now fully recovered from the devastation of war. Their economies were now far stronger and more productive than at prewar levels. Indeed, West Germany and Japan in particular had replaced older, obsolete plants and equipment with technologically advanced systems. Labor costs were considerably lower than in the United States. The United States had seemingly lost its competitive edge.

For the first time since 1893, the United States in 1970 bought more goods than it sold abroad. Except for 1973 and 1975, the trade imbalance continued to grow. In 1980 the United States experienced a $40 billion trade imbalance, and five years later the imbalance was $140 billion. The growing imbalance of trade between the United States and its partners after 1971 did not reflect a decline in U.S. productivity so much as being evidence of the rising vigor of the

Japanese, European, and British economies. As those economies produced more goods and services, consumers within those regions depended less on the import of American products and services. And conversely, American consumers began to find that foreign-made products were often less expensive and of equal or superior quality to American-made products. American auto manufacturers in particular began to lose a portion of the domestic market to smaller, more fuel-efficient and often lower-priced imports. Volkswagens from West Germany were the favored import in the 1960s, Hondas and Nissan Sentras took the lead in the 1970s. American manufacturers began losing market share to foreign competitors at home and abroad.

The U.S. share of total world trade in manufactured goods declined from about 23 percent to 16 percent. In 1971, West Germany sold more manufactured goods in the world markets than did the United States. Japan's portion of the global market rose from 6 percent in 1960 to about 13 percent in 1971. A strong U.S. dollar contributed to the trade imbalance. Foreign manufactured goods were bargains given the value of the dollar compared to the currencies of other nations. The trade imbalance aggravated American financial pressures—and helped force devaluation of the dollar. The federal debt rose at the same time that the ability to service that debt (that is, as income into the economy from foreign sales) began to decline. Small wonder that the dollar came under increasing pressure as a reserve currency.

The International Monetary Fund (IMF) responded to the problem in 1970 by introducing a new reserve currency or asset called special drawing rights (SDRs), which were unconditional rights to draw on foreign currencies managed by the IMF. The IMF would thus function as a world trade bank, with the assets of the bank being "deposits" by member countries. Trading partners could in effect draw upon each other's currencies depending on the amount of trade conducted with those partners. The SDRs, however, continued to have an uncertain value and stability, while gold and the dollar received preference.

Rising inflation in the United States reflected the underlying trade, debt, and federal spending situation. Inflation became a vexing problem. Wholesale prices rose from an average base of 100 in 1967 to 119 in 1972, 135 in 1973, and 150 in 1974. Unemployment rolls jumped from less than 3 million in 1969 to almost 5 million in 1971. Meanwhile, the U.S. stock of gold held in reserve for international exchange declined to $11 billion, only a fraction of that needed to meet outstanding obligations to nations holding dollars. In August 1971 President Richard M. Nixon announced a ninety-day wage, price, and rent freeze in an unprecedented effort to halt inflation. He also announced that the United States would no longer buy and sell gold at $35 dollars an ounce. This freed the dollar from its gold valuation and halted the conversion of foreign-held dollars into gold. That action made the SDRs a more palatable, but still imperfect, reserve currency.

In Phase II of the domestic price freeze initiated by President Nixon, federal boards were appointed to monitor wage and price increases, and prices were to be gradually decontrolled. Inflation was in fact slowed, but unemployment remained high and American trade deficits continued to rise. Inflation was met in part by devaluing the dollar. The United States could pay its debts in cheaper dollars. In December, the president announced an 8.57 percent devaluation of the dollar, which raised the price of gold to $38 per ounce. Over time the dollar and SDRs were technically freed from any gold valuation and gold floated free as a market commodity. On January 1, 1975, American citizens were allowed to buy, sell, and own gold for the first time since 1934. But in the interim, the problem with the dollar and inflation refused to go away.

Devaluation of the dollar in theory made the American market more attractive to foreign consumers, thus promoting American exports. Despite the devaluation, the trade deficit did not improve but only seemed to worsen. President Nixon's administration initiated a new diplomacy that sought detente with the Soviet Union and other Cold War adversaries as a way both to contain the spread of war and insurrection in Vietnam, Pakistan, and the Middle East, thus reducing American defense costs, and as an initiative to open new global markets for American products. Nixon visited Peking in February 1972 and Moscow in May. A direct result of the new detente policies may have been the conclusion of large grain sales to the Soviet Union and Nixon's reelection to the presidency.

American trade balances began to show signs of improvement, and in January 1973 all mandatory wage and price controls were lifted. In February of that year, the United States announced a further 10 percent devaluation of the dollar and subsequently allowed the dollar to float free in international markets. The economy was stimulated by massive foreign grain sales that resulted in soaring domestic wheat, grain, and meat prices—and a new trigger to an inflationary spiral. One result, critics pointed out, was that the Soviet Union executed a financial coup in purchasing American wheat for $3 a bushel and selling it back to us or others for $6. The administration imposed new ceilings on wholesale and retail meat prices. In June 1973, the administration clamped a freeze on retail prices excluding rent, interest, dividends, and raw agricultural products. Stability and recovery seemed to be returning. But in mid-1973, the United States and most global markets suffered a much more serious disruption.

THE OPEC EMBARGO

An oil embargo imposed by OPEC nations created an energy crisis. That in turn had global financial repercussions. As almost every business index began to show improvement in mid-1973, a total ban on oil exports to the United States by the OPEC nations created severe energy and monetary crises in the United States and elsewhere. In 1960, when OPEC was formed following a collective decision by producers in the Mideast to reduce the price paid for oil, five major U.S. oil companies accounted for almost two-thirds of the world's petroleum production. U.S. companies produced most of the world's petroleum and the United States consumed most of the world's petroleum. Generally, between 1955 and 1970, crude petroleum sold at $2 to $3 per barrel. Cheap fuel coupled with rapid expansion in the petrochemical industry (plastics, paints, insecticides, synthetic fibers) combined to raise U.S. and global consumption of petroleum dramatically. Domestic production actually rose from 2.5 to 3.5 billion barrels (42-gal/bbl) between 1960 and 1970, but consumption rose more rapidly. Once a major exporter of petroleum, the United States now relied more heavily on imports to meet its own needs. During the decade, imports rose from 371 to 483 million barrels. Most of the imported oil came from OPEC production.

Politics, rather than economics, triggered the first embargo. The establishment of the state of Israel following the close of World War II had created continuing strife between Israel and its Arab neighbors. In 1967, during the Six Day War, Israel seized Egyptian and Syrian territories, including the controversial Sinai Peninsula, Arab East Jerusalem and the West Bank, and the Golan Heights, thereby enlarging its territory by four times the original 1949 boundaries. Syria, Egypt, and the Arab world chafed under the apparent Western concurrence with the seizures and maintained rising pressures on Israel. In October 1973, new fighting broke out between Israel and the Arab states. The United States, with the support of the Soviet Union, arranged a speedy truce. In an effort to win their objectives by means other than war, the Arab (OPEC) nations followed the truce with an embargo on the shipment of oil to the United States, Japan, and most of Western Europe. The idea was to force Western nations, particularly the United States, to force Israel to withdraw from Arab territories occupied during the Six Day War.

The embargo had an impact far greater than any imagined. A worldwide energy crisis ensued. The crisis shocked the U.S. economy, which since 1958 had become energy dependent. By 1973, one-third of the petroleum consumed in the United States was imported, most of that from the Middle East. American transportation relied upon oil and gasoline. Electric generating plants used fuel oil and natural gas. Agriculture relied on petrochemicals for fertilizers and upon gasoline for cultivation. The embargo meant a traumatic rise in the costs of manufacturing, transportation, and food production. Household expenses soared. Gasoline, which averaged 30 cents per gallon or so in 1973, more than doubled in price in a few weeks and continued to climb. Household utility bills tripled; food prices soared. Secretary of State Henry Kissinger succeeded in negotiating a temporary settlement and a lifting of the embargo by convincing Israel to withdraw from part of the occupied territories. But the energy crisis had only begun. The OPEC nations, directed largely by Saudi Arabia's remarkable Abdullah Tariki, seized upon petroleum as the essential instrument of global diplomacy. For the following decade "oil power," rather than the more traditional seapower or airpower, dominated global policies.

Tariki, from Saudi Arabia, obtained a B.S. degree in geology from the University of Cairo in 1945 and an M.A. in petroleum geology from the University of Texas in 1947 before joining Texaco. After training with Texaco, he returned to Saudi Arabia to head the inspection office of the Bureau of Mines and became Director General of Petroleum and Mineral Resources in 1954. In 1960, he became Minister of Petroleum and Mineral Resources. He fought vigorously against what he termed "discriminatory pricing" by Western oil interests (ARAMCO). With the clear successes scored by the embargo in 1973 that was initiated as a political device, Tariki and OPEC seized upon petroleum as a tool for implementing economic changes. Although lifting the embargo, OPEC announced that OPEC crude—

Sheik Abdullah Tariki, trained in geology at the University of Texas, became Saudi Arabia's Minister of Petroleum and Mineral Resources in 1960, and architect of the Organization of Petroleum Exporting Countries (OPEC). OPEC has impacted heavily on world trade and commerce since a petroleum embargo in 1973.

(AP/Wide World Photos)

and hence world prices—would rise to $11.65 a barrel. They did. And more.

Over the next five or six years, crude oil prices rose almost 1700 percent. Petroleum that sold for $2 per barrel cost $32.50 in 1980. Despite long lines at filling stations, brownouts, and stiff price rises in almost all consumer goods, the U.S. dependence on imported oil grew rather than diminished.

American companies vigorously pursued sources for new domestic production. Improved drilling and extraction processes were developed. Alternative fuels, wind generators, solar cells, grain alcohol fuel supplements, lower-grade carbon fuels such as lignite, smaller automobiles and more efficient engines, and better generators and heating and cooling apparatuses were sought. The United States attempted to become energy efficient, while petroleum imports continued to climb. By 1977, when Alaska North Slope oil came on line, almost one-half of U.S. petroleum consumption came from imported oil. More than 70 percent of imported oil came from OPEC. (See Table 6-1)

Because of the escalation in crude petroleum prices, the United States and other Western nations including Japan, which depended almost entirely on petroleum imports, transferred billions of dollars of their wealth to the OPEC nations. Even within the United States, a

TABLE 6-1

Crude Oil and Petroleum Product Imports by Country of Origin, 1960–1985 (Thousand Barrels per Day)

| | ORGANIZATION OF PETROLEUM EXPORTING COUNTRIES (OPEC)[1] | | | | | | | | | | | | | | |
Year	Algeria	Indonesia	Nigeria	Saudi Arabia	Venezuela	Other OPEC[2]	Total OPEC[3]	Arab Members of OPEC[4]	Canada	Mexico	United Kingdom	Virgin Is. and Puerto Rico	Other Non-OPEC	Total	OPEC Oil as Percent of Total Imports
1960	1	77	0	84	911	241	1,314	292	120	16	(5)	36	328	1,815	72
1961	0	62	0	73	879	272	1,286	284	190	40	1	44	357	1,917	67
1962	0	69	0	74	906	216	1,265	241	250	49	2	41	475	2,082	61
1963	1	63	0	108	900	211	1,283	258	265	48	3	44	480	2,123	60
1964	6	68	0	131	933	223	1,361	293	299	47	(5)	47	505	2,259	60
1965	9	63	15	158	994	237	1,476	324	323	48	(5)	47	574	2,468	60
1966	4	53	11	147	1,018	238	1,471	300	384	45	6	61	606	2,573	57
1967	5	66	5	92	938	153	1,259	177	450	49	11	96	673	2,537	50
1968	6	73	9	74	886	255	1,302	272	506	45	28	145	814	2,840	46
1969	2	88	49	65	875	256	1,336	276	608	43	20	189	971	3,166	42
1970	8	70	50	30	989	197	1,343	196	766	42	11	271	985	3,419	39
1971	15	111	102	128	1,020	296	1,673	327	857	27	10	368	991	3,926	43
1972	92	164	251	190	959	406	2,063	530	1,108	21	9	432	1,108	4,741	44
1973	136	213	459	486	1,135	564	2,993	915	1,325	16	15	429	1,479	6,256	48
1974	190	300	713	461	979	635	3,280	752	1,070	8	8	481	1,265	6,112	54
1975	282	390	762	715	702	750	3,601	1,383	846	71	14	496	1,026	6,056	59
1976	432	539	1,025	1,230	700	1,140	5,066	2,424	599	87	31	510	1,019	7,313	69
1977	559	541	1,143	1,380	690	1,880	6,193	3,185	517	179	126	571	1,221	8,807	70
1978	649	573	919	1,144	645	1,821	5,751	2,963	467	318	180	522	1,126	8,363	69
1979	636	420	1,080	1,356	690	1,456	5,637	3,056	538	439	202	523	1,116	8,456	67
1980	488	348	857	1,261	481	865	4,300	2,551	455	533	176	476	969	6,909	62
1981	311	366	620	1,129	406	491	3,323	1,848	447	522	375	389	939	5,996	55
1982	170	248	514	552	412	250	2,146	854	482	685	456	366	979	5,113	42
1983	240	338	302	337	422	223	1,862	632	547	826	382	322	1,111	5,051	37
1984	323	343	216	325	548	294	2,049	819	630	748	402	336	1,273	5,437	38
1985	187	314	293	168	605	264	1,830	472	770	816	310	275	1,066	5,067	36

[1] See Glossary for membership.

[2] Includes Ecuador, Gabon, Iran, Iraq, Kuwait, Libya, Qatar, and United Arab Emirates.

[3] Includes petroleum imported into the United States indirectly from OPEC countries, primarily from Caribbean and West European refining areas, as petroleum products which were refined from crude oil produced in OPEC countries.

[4] Includes Algeria, Iraq, Kuwait, Libya, Qatar, Saudi Arabia, and United Arab Emirates.

[5] Less than 500 barrels per day.

Note: Data include imports for the Strategic Petroleum Reserve, which began in 1977.

Note: Sum of components may not equal total due to independent rounding.

SOURCES: •1960 through 1975—Bureau of Mines, Minerals Yearbook; "Crude Petroleum and Petroleum Products" Chapter. •1976 through 1980—Energy Information Administration, Energy Data Reports, P.A.D. Districts Supply/Demand, Annual. •1981 through 1985—Energy Information Administration, Petroleum Supply Annual. •See Energy Information Administration, Annual Energy Review, 1987, Table 49, p. 113.

transfer of money occurred from the energy-dependent states to the energy-producing states. Alaska, California, and Texas, for example, were beneficiaries of the embargo. The transfer of capital caused even greater financial problems among the Western economies, already in turmoil because of the weakening dollar and the demonetization of gold.

In 1973, the IMF had attempted to improve the credibility of the special drawing rights by adopting a fixed relation to the dollar, while maintaining a floating exchange rate for other currencies with the SDR. The continuing deterioration of the dollar led, in 1974, to the IMF adopting a basket valuation for the SDR—linking the U.S. dollar, German mark, Japanese yen, French franc, and British pound to the SDR. By linking the world's strongest currencies to a single reserve currency, the SDR, the IMF freed international exchange from its now precarious dependence on the dollar and devised a new, stable, and equitable base for international exchange. Gold, meanwhile, became (in theory) simply another commodity. In practice, of course, the "gold tradition" continued to lead investors and speculators to gold as a financial hedge. On January 1, 1975, Congress repealed the law prohibiting private ownership of gold in the United States and the U.S. Treasury began auctioning its surplus gold. On the same day, the IMF abolished gold as the base unit for international exchange and began auctioning one-sixth of its supplies at market prices with profits to go to less-developed nations. Thus, in 1975, at least in theory, world trade was detached from gold perhaps for the first time since the days of King Midas (whenever that was).

That helped, but it did not solve the energy crisis nor resolve the U.S. dwindling balance of trade. In 1971, even before the OPEC embargo, the United States experienced its first trade deficit; that is, it bought more than it sold for the first time since 1893. In 1975, perhaps in part due to the demonetization of gold, the end of the Vietnam War, and to inflation that increased the cost of foreign goods in the United States, the United States experienced an improvement in its balance of trade, enjoying a $9 billion surplus compared to the $2 billion surplus in 1970. (Because of inflation, however, the $9 billion would have been about $5 billion in 1970 dollars.) The improvement proved to be only fleeting. By 1980, the United States was running a $25 billion deficit.

The demonetization of gold and the inflation of the dollar had been expected to improve the balance of payments. It had not. Inflation should have raised the cost of foreign-made products to the

American consumer and thus slowed imports, while effectively lowering the cost of U.S. products abroad and encouraging exports.
Inflation possibly had that result. But it did more. Inflation resulted
in higher interest rates for investment capital. Capital became more
scarce. The lack of investment capital and the higher costs of
the capital reduced productivity. Declining productivity promoted
higher inflation. The weaker dollar raised prices paid for foreign
products, including petroleum. The balance of trade worsened, and
inflation rose in response. The economy seemed to be stuck in a new
inflationary spiral. But there was more, inflation aside.

U.S. sales abroad (that is, the American share of the global market) was declining. Exports of manufactured goods had been in a
steep decline since about 1967, and the U.S. share of high-technology
exports, particularly electronics, had drifted lower since 1967. This
occurred while American imports of not only petroleum, but also
automobiles, electronics, and clothing climbed. By 1980, among the
ten best-selling automobiles in America were the Honda, the Hyun-
dai, and the Nissan Sentra. The problems with the American economy did not wholly relate to the OPEC embargo, war and defense
spending, increased spending by the federal government for social
programs, the recovery of European and the Japanese economies, or
the demise of the dollar as the world's reserve currency. There was
something more.

THE NEW REALITY: GLOBAL COMPETITION

A sense of unease about the economy grew throughout the decade
of the 1970s, yet there was no clear definition about the problem.
The economy continued to grow, as did inflation and unemployment
in many industries. By 1980, the number of workers employed by
the American steel industry had declined by more than one-half from
the 1970 level. But in other industries such as computers and electronics, opportunities and expansion appeared to be strong. Agricultural exports and farm prices continued to grow throughout the
1970s, in a few years exceeding the export of manufactured goods.
But overall, imports were rising sharply, while exports declined. The
export of farm products reached a plateau in the early 1980s. The
export of manufactured goods continued to decline. American public and private spending soared, particularly between 1975 and 1980.

The trade imbalance grew, as did the federal deficit. Managed inflation and budget and tax revisions failed to stimulate or correct the problems. Growth in GNP, and in personal income, although indicated by the numbers, seemed to be eaten up by inflation. The economy was in a state, some said, of "stagflation."

"Churning" might have been a word to apply to the economy. There was considerable activity in the financial community. The outflow of capital caused by the energy crisis seemed to be correcting. New capital was coming into the country, particularly "petrodollars" from Saudi Arabia and other OPEC nations. Those petrodollars were the profits from selling what had once been $2 per barrel crude at $12, $16, and finally $32.50 per barrel. It was, to an extent, American money coming back home. But it no longer belonged to Americans. Almost unnoticed until the end of the decade, Japanese investors began to make substantial capital investments in American banking, real estate, and financial instruments. British investors, even less visibly but with no less vigor, poured new capital into the American economy. By the close of the decade America's financial centers were enjoying an aura of well-being. But manufacturers, farmers, workers, and consumers felt uneasy and experienced discomfort but lacked a sense of focus or direction. America's awakening to a new economic reality was slow.

Journalists and economists began to register an unease that went beyond the usual liberal versus conservative rhetoric. A lead article in the September 1980 *Atlantic Monthly,* for example, looked at "American Industry: What Ails It, How to Save It." The story began with an account of a vacation trip by recently elected U.S. Senator John Danforth (R–MO) and his wife Sally to Europe in 1977. "Everywhere they went they encountered prosperous travelers from Japan." They were at the Louvre, at the Gucci shops, everywhere, doing the same thing—buying! "Something's going on!" Danforth told his wife. *Atlantic Monthly*'s author voiced the radical and perverse thought that "the American era of economic domination may be nearing its eclipse."

Evidence of the end of that economic domination, even within the Western hemisphere, seemed to many Americans to be born out by the decision to transfer the Panama Canal from American control to that of the government of Panama. A right-of-way through the Isthmus of Panama had been obtained by the United States in a treaty with the newly created Republic of Panama in 1903. It was considered the hallmark of Theodore Roosevelt's presidency and

The Panama Canal

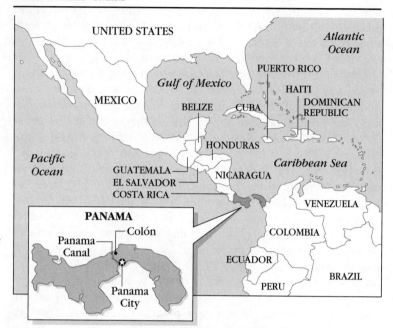

The Panama Canal, completed by the United States in 1914, is one of the great international waterways of the world with a history that dates back to the sixteenth century. In 1977, reflecting in part the decline of American economic hegemony, a growing sense of hemispheric cooperation, and the fact that the canal could no longer accommodate many of the larger warships and freighters, the United States agreed to a treaty with the Republic of Panama granting sovereignty over the canal to Panama with control to follow in the year 2000.

evidence of the new global stature being attained by the United States. The construction of the Canal by the Corps of Engineers under the direction of Colonel George W. Goethals was considered one of the great engineering achievements of all time. The Canal opened in 1914 and became one of the world's most important commercial waterways, proving critical in American naval defense in both world wars.

In the 1970s Panamanians began agitating for the return of the Canal to Panamanian sovereignty and control. Other Latin American nations regarded American control of the Canal as imperialistic and evidence of America's disregard for the national rights of the American republics. The United States, sensitive to the charges of imperialism and fresh from defeat in Vietnam, was sensitive to the charges. In addition, the Canal now had logistic limitations. It could not handle the large supercarriers and supertankers being used by the United States and other maritime nations. The Canal was expensive to operate and became a political liability. In 1977 the United States and Panama ratified two treaties, one of which immediately conveyed sovereignty over the Panama Canal to the Republic of Panama while the other provided that possession and control over the Canal would pass to Panama by the year 2000. Although transfer of the Canal may have been correct and expedient, Americans sensed, given the time and seeming decline of American competitiveness, that the United States was losing global stature.

Politicians talked of a new partnership with business to "reindustrialize" America, editorialists lamented the loss of America's will and ability to produce, economists offered "theoretical explications" of a greater truth, manufacturers blamed labor, labor blamed business, academics blamed everybody, everybody faulted government, and government accused its trading partners of unfair competition. Fall 1980, perhaps like fall 1932, marked a "winter of American discontent."

The general disaffection and concern, still largely unfocused, led to the election of Republican President Ronald Reagan, and a turn not so much to the "right" as in a new direction. The federal government instituted what were nominally "austerity" measures, including tax and spending reductions and deregulation of industries (primarily communications, transportation, and utilities) designed to stimulate more production and lower costs. Trade policies were eased and tight monetary policies imposed.

The results seemed to be, in the short term, rising unemployment, larger trade deficits, larger federal budget deficits, and declining economic growth. A recession in 1981 to 1983 created hard times. But imports declined, the dollar strengthened, and inflation fell sharply from its high of near 13 percent annually to a more manageable 3–4 percent level. Petroleum prices also fell rapidly, settling to about $18 a barrel, then declining to $12.50 by 1986. Beginning in 1978, American consumers began using the 650 million barrels pumped annually from the Alaska North Slope oil fields. America's energy crisis seemed to be over. Paradoxically, the rapid fall of petroleum prices created a new round of financial destabilization in the American petroleum industry, in banking, and in the oil-producing regions of the United States—including Alaska. The energy crisis may have been solved, but a deeper and more pervasive economic ailment had not.

Something was going on outside of the United States. By 1973, the United Kingdom, Ireland, and Denmark had joined Belgium, France, Italy, Luxembourg, the Netherlands, and West Germany in the European Community (EC). Greece joined in 1981, and Spain and Portugal followed during the decade. By 1968, under a timetable set in 1957, the European Community had established itself as a free trade zone, eliminating all restrictions on trade in manufactured goods (but not agricultural products) among member nations. By 1970, the European Community had raised its value of industrial product by five times the 1957 level and offered a common external tariff system. Beginning in 1980, the EC began integrating its internal markets more fully; that is, eliminating customs regulations, red tape, contradictions in laws, and financial impediments to trade. By 1980, the United States no longer competed internationally with the independent nations of Europe, but with a new integrated European Economic Community. The implications of that were not fully apparent in the United States. The rhetoric of national leaders in Europe was still traditional nationalistic rhetoric, but the reality was quite different.

Nor had the United States fully come to grasp that the "Japanese miracle" had imperceptibly changed American business relations with Japan. While the United States remained the dominant economic partner, it was by no means as powerful or as dominant as in the past. Only slowly did American business realize that the "economic miracle" had also begun to permeate Southeast Asia. South Korea had become a major producer and exporter of automobiles, air conditioners, and electronics. Hong Kong, long a thriving commercial center under British authority, had become an international trading center. Canton, China; Bangkok, Thailand; and Singapore, Malaysia, began to creep into the American geographical comprehension. When one visited those areas of the world, once so remote to the United States and its interests, the sense of global business, commerce, and industry became immediately evident. Without Americans having fully realized it, over the past two decades "the global economy has been transformed around us." And the United States had not fully participated in that transformation despite its seeming intensive involvement in global affairs through its defense and foreign aid programs.

In June 1983, President Ronald Reagan appointed a special presidential Commission on Industrial Competitiveness, to study "the new reality of global competition faced by American industry, both at home and abroad." The problems recognized by the commission were that American business's ability to compete in world markets was eroding. Growth in U.S. productivity lagged far behind that of foreign competitors. Real wages in the United States were not improving. Returns on assets invested in manufacturing were so poor as to discourage investment and expansion in manufacturing.

Perhaps the best understanding as to what global competitiveness meant, the commission reasoned, was to understand what competitiveness was *not*. Being competitive did not mean maintaining a favorable balance of trade. Even the poorest nations could sell more than they bought, but remain poor. It did not even mean increasing employment in the manufacturing sector. Japan, for example, while increasing its competitiveness in the world had seen manufacturing decline by 25 to 35 percent of its GNP. Global competitiveness did not mean maintaining the viability of all manufacturing industries. "While competitiveness does not require the success of any particular industry, it is in the U.S. national interest to maintain a broad and diverse industrial base in which many industries achieve high levels of productivity," the report concluded.

One key to gauging global competitiveness was the gross domestic product per employed person. How did that productivity compare to the productivity of other nations? Between 1973 and 1983 the real gross domestic product per employed person in the United States was only one-seventh that of its major trading partners. Real wages paid American workers rose steadily at an annual rate of 2.6 percent between 1963 and 1973, but became essentially stagnant for the next decade. The industrial economy had in recent years failed to support an increase in the standard of living of American workers. Returns on investments in manufacturing had fallen behind returns on investments in passive financial assets such as stocks and bonds. The U.S. merchandise trade balance had been in decline (except for 1973 and 1975) since 1967. U.S. firms were no longer producing products that met the test of international markets.

Concurrently, the American position in the world economy had fundamentally changed. The world had become wealthier and more interdependent. Trade occupied a larger portion of each nation's GNP. Foreign trade accounted for an increasingly larger part of American income. Trade as a percentage of GNP in the United States doubled from 7 percent in 1960 to 14 percent in 1983. American products sold abroad and the American purchase of products manufactured overseas had become increasingly sensitive to changes in the international marketplace. The American domestic economy no longer drove the engine of world commerce as it once did. American consumers no longer consumed most of the world's product, and thus set the market for global trade. Once positioned above competition, American technology now confronted heavy competition, in part because the pace of technological change increased rapidly in Europe and in Asia, while the United States rested upon its seemingly commanding lead. American industry focused on the still seemingly insatiable and still profitable domestic market, a market which, coincidentally, was much more accessible and much more comprehensible and manageable than foreign markets or the global market.

While the United States had been singularly successful in Americanizing the world economy between 1945 and 1970, restructuring the American economy for that new global environment after 1970 proved to be a difficult and often painful process.

Chapter 7

Coping with Change

The problem of restructuring American business to meet the challenges of the new global environment had as much to do with changing attitudes and ideas as it did with technological innovation or retooling. American society, as much as American business had an attitude problem. Americans simply could not perceive or accept the new reality of the changed status of the United States within the global community. The United States had been inordinately successful in its mission to change the world following World War II. The American crusade for democracy and the defense of democratic institutions throughout the global community had, Americans believed, revolutionized the world and changed it for a better and more just society.

But it was not really democracy at work changing the world, suggested David Potter, professor of history at Yale University, in his fascinating 1954 examination of *People of Plenty: Economic Abundance and the American Character;* rather, it was American-made abundance that was revolutionizing the world. It was a process that had begun much earlier. In 1932 a French businessman suggested that the Western message of spirituality (that is, virtue and goodness) that it attempted to spread throughout the globe was really not the message received by the global community. Rather, he said, what was borrowed were the West's mechanisms. "Today, in the most remote, most ancient villages, one finds the automobile, the cinema, the radio, the telephone, the phonograph, not to mention the airplane, and it is not the white men, nor the most civilized, who display the greatest enthusiasm for them." And the businessman went on to comment, almost prophetically, "The United States is presiding at a general reorganization of the ways of living throughout the entire world."

After World War II America's message to the world, at least the message received by the global community, was again not ideological (that is, democratic), but rather material. The message of materialism was itself not new. Colonial powers had broadcast the message of commerce and business for centuries. But the colonial powers traditionally practiced imperialism for the purpose of supplying their own material needs. On the contrary, the United States, through the Marshall Plan and its investment and spending policies in general, disseminated the belief that abundance could actually be placed within the grasp of ordinary men and women the world over. That, rather than democracy, was the revolutionary message that America communicated to the world. That was the message that ultimately changed the world and continued to revolutionize government and human affairs for the remainder of the twentieth century. Thus, it was not democracy that was revolutionizing the world, but the idea that "freedom from want" and even abundance could be attained by the ordinary individual throughout the world.

Even as the world changed about them, Americans failed to fully comprehend the causes and the nature of that change. It had to do with materialism and capitalism more than democracy, although they were related. Capitalism American-style was based upon the value and worth of the individual. It genuinely assumed that each person had a right to earn according to their ability and that an open society and free trade made it possible for the individual to earn and to achieve. But in helping create a "free world," the United States also helped create a global market based on free trade and a world ever more competitive. That competition began to change the way Americans did business at home and abroad.

COPING WITH COMPETITION

American reaction to the increasing evidence of competition from abroad generally followed a classical psychological pattern: 1) ignore it, 2) discount it, 3) repulse it, 4) acknowledge it, and 5) adapt to it. For example, the United States produced almost one-half of the world's steel through the 1950s. It had the largest, most efficient steel plants, and American steel workers enjoyed the world's highest wage rates. The United States was both the leading consumer and the leading exporter of iron and steel products, including automobiles. American auto manufacturers enjoyed a half-century of production experience, a skilled and well-paid labor force, and low-cost raw materials. The iron and steel industry, closely related to auto manufacturing, had access to relatively abundant and cheap raw materials and energy. However, the world status of American steel and automobile manufacture changed dramatically between 1950 and 1970.

While American automobile production remained remarkably stable, averaging 6.2 to 6.7 million vehicles annually, the American share of world motor vehicle production dropped from 78 percent to 31 percent. Beginning about 1962 the United States began buying more iron and steel products from abroad than it exported, and by 1968, Americans were buying more automobiles from foreign manufacturers than were being sold overseas. During the 1970s Honda-, Hyundai-, and Nissan-produced vehicles moved among the top ten in domestic auto sales. Japan's modernization of its iron and steel processes and international marketing were basic to the expansion of its automotive industry.

Japanese production costs for a ton of steel improved dramatically in comparison to U.S. costs during the 1960s and 1970s. Between 1950 and 1971 Japan completed construction of eleven steel mills with a combined production capacity of 115 thousand metric tons of steel. During the same period, the United States opened two new steel mills with a combined capacity of 11 thousand metric tons. In 1970, most American steel furnaces were open-hearth furnaces built before World War II. Furnaces had an average production capacity of less than one million tons. Japan's plants, on the other hand, were the more modern and efficient basic oxygen furnaces which utilized continuous slab or billet casting. U.S. steel manufacture relied on the older ingot production, with the ingots then being rolled or milled into manufacturing stock called slabs, billets, or blooms. Continuous casting in effect eliminated a stage in metal production and reduced costs. The larger blast furnaces used by Japanese manufacturers to produce pig iron resulted in 30 percent savings in the cost of pig iron—the basic ingredient in steel.

Japanese steel manufacturers compensated for the lack of the domestic raw materials used in the production of iron and steel (that is, iron ore and coal) by investing in new mine operations at high-purity, high-production operations throughout the world, primarily in Australia and Canada. Production costs were generally lower in these new operations because of the higher-grade ores and the use of improved strip mining and harvest operations, but those costs were offset by the high costs of transporting the raw materials to the mills in Japan. Transportation costs in turn were lowered by investment in deep-water ports and super-cargo-sized ships.

Japanese steel manufacturers enjoyed relatively lower-cost labor than American producers, but during the period of most rapid Japanese expansion, industry wages in Japan rose from being approximately 12 percent of those paid in the United States to 58 percent of those paid in the United States. Other benefits provided Japanese workers meant that real wages for Japanese workers by 1979 averaged 70 percent of the levels paid U.S. steel makers. Japanese manufacturers did enjoy lower labor costs than U.S. manufacturers, but those were not sufficient to offset other cost advantages acquired by Japanese steel.

Despite the growing competitiveness of Japanese steel with American industry, American manufacturers and the general public well into the 1970s believed U.S. steel technology to be superior to that of any other country, its steel of better quality, and its prices competitive. U.S. steel manufacture did expand throughout the 1960s and 1970s. New investment in manufacturing processes totaled some $60 billion between 1950 and 1979. For the most part, however, that investment was based on improving the returns on existing plants and equipment, rather than on modernization. More efficient and higher production facilities such as continuous casting and higher speed rolling mills were linked to older, low-production blast furnaces, which failed to provide the volume needed to realize the improved efficiencies of new processes.

Most of the expansion and modernization of Japan's steel manufacturing processes occurred between 1966 and 1972, when Japanese industry increased its investment in production assets by an average 23 percent a year. During the same years, U.S. manufacturers increased production assets by only 4 percent per year. Meanwhile, U.S. steel enjoyed a 3.8 percent return on investments, compared to a 1.8 percent return for Japanese steel investments. American profits in steel continued relatively high compared to Japanese profits. American industry leaders and the public assumed that the United States continued to enjoy a competitive advantage of foreign steel manufacturers.

But the basic facts were that by 1970 American auto manufacturers had to pay 25 to 30 percent more for their steel than did Japanese manufacturers. American steel was losing its world market. For perhaps the first time since the 1850s Americans were importing more iron and steel products than they were selling abroad. Americans were buying more foreign-made automobiles and selling fewer American-made automobiles overseas.

By 1970, the stage of denial that the United States faced a problem in its steel industry passed into the "discounting" phase. The steel and auto problem was temporary, it was believed. The declining value of the dollar meant that American products (including iron, steel, and automobiles) would be more competitively priced abroad and thus sales would rise markedly. Conversely, the cheaper dollar meant that Japanese automobiles sold in America would return lower profits to Japanese manufacturers and thus reduce the competitiveness of Japanese vehicles. (In other words, a Honda that sold for $10,000 in the United States when the American dollar was valued at 250 yen would produce 2.5 million yen, while a $10,000 sale at 200 yen would produce only 2.0 million yen.) But despite devaluation, the sale of Japanese automobiles in the United States continued to rise, while the sale of American automobiles in Japan and elsewhere declined. American auto manufacturers continued to lose both domestic and global auto sales share to foreign competitors.

Devaluation actually resulted in lowering some of the production costs for Japanese manufacturers, despite the lower profits from sales of units in the United States. Raw materials and energy costs most directly affected by the value of the dollar declined somewhat, thus despite a 5 or 10 percent devaluation of the dollar in relation to the yen, devaluation cost Japan manufacturers only a 1 or 2 percent loss in their profit margin.

American business leaders and the general public then began to accuse Japan of unfair competition (the repulse stage), and blamed low tariffs in the United States, higher American labor costs, and the added costs of environmental legislation for the lack of American competitiveness. Federal debts and federal deficits were blamed, as was the failure by industry to spend enough on research and development. Education was faulted for failing to train enough engineers. Japanese universities produced twice as many engineers each year as did American universities. Pressures began to mount on Congress to open the Japanese market, restrict Japanese access to the American market, relax pollution and environmental controls, and to provide

TABLE 7-1

World Production of Motor Vehicles and Steel

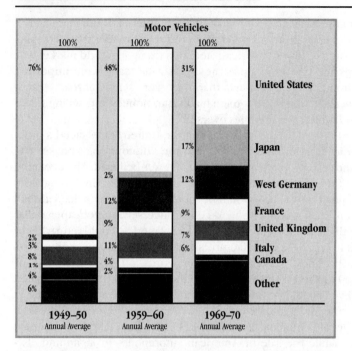

Motor Vehicles

	1949–50 Annual Average	1959–60 Annual Average	1969–70 Annual Average	
	100%	100%	100%	
United States	76%	48%	31%	
Japan			17%	
West Germany		2%	12%	
France		12%	9%	
United Kingdom	2%	9%	7%	
Italy	3%	11%	6%	
Canada	8%	4%		
	1%	2%		
Other	4%			
	6%			

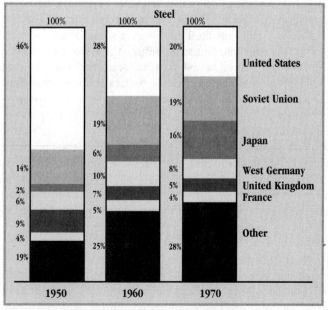

Steel

	1950	1960	1970
	100%	100%	100%
United States	46%	28%	20%
Soviet Union			19%
Japan	14%	19%	16%
West Germany		6%	8%
United Kingdom	2%	10%	5%
France	6%	7%	4%
	9%	5%	
Other	4%	25%	28%
	19%		

Source: The United States in the Changing World Economy, Council on International Economic Policy, December 27, 1971, Chart 9.

greater investment incentives and faster tax depreciation to enhance profits. The American response to the awareness of growing global competition generally did not include massive development in new plants and equipment, or more aggressive overseas marketing. Only with reluctance did American auto manufacturers begin to produce smaller, lighter, and more fuel-efficient automobiles that could be marketed in direct competition with imports.

American industry continued to focus on maximizing short-term returns on existing capital investment (plants and equipment), rather than on long-term competitiveness that would involve large capital outlays and, for at least a time, lowered returns on invested capital. To an extent, European steel and auto manufacturers shared America's declining competitiveness. European steel plants, however, largely destroyed during World War II, had been rebuilt with more modern manufacturing processes than used by the older American mills. Also, Europe was able to partially compensate for the greater competition from Japanese producers by creating cost savings and market advantages by creating the European Common Market. The United States remained independent and alone. To be sure, the United States still produced and purchased a major share of the world's iron, steel, and automotive products. That continuing perception of the dominance of the American economy, perhaps understandably, caused American industry to be preoccupied with American production and American markets. It took time before global competition became a part of American business's "New Reality." The reality that the United States was in fact not dominant in the global economy became startlingly clear in the television and electronics industry.

TELEVISION AND ELECTRONICS

The modern television and electronics industries are extensions of radio industries established at the turn of the century. An understanding of the contemporary globalization of the communications industry, and of America's role in that process, requires a review of the development of radio. Radio, or wireless telegraphy, grew out of telegraph systems perfected by Samuel F. B. Morse before the American Civil War and from the theory of electromagnetic waves propounded by James Clerk Maxwell, a British physicist, in 1873. There were no successful experiments or proof until Guglielmo Marconi, an Italian electrical engineer, began experimenting with "wireless" telegraphy in 1890. He successfully directed a radio signal to a receiver several kilometers away from his antenna in 1895. He patented his system and formed the Marconi Wireless Telegraph Company, Ltd., in London in 1897. In 1899 radio signals could be sent across the English Channel between Great Britain and France, and in 1901, signals were successfully directed across the Atlantic to Newfoundland, Canada. Regular transatlantic wireless service began in 1907.

Following the sinking of the *Titanic,* the United States began to require radio operators on all American ships. By World War I, most armies and navies of the world had adopted radio as standard communication equipment. The concurrent development of the incandescent bulb by Thomas A. Edison and the perfection of diode (or two element tubes), followed by the three-element cathode tube perfected by Lee De Forest in 1906, enabled the transmission of voices and sound (rather than telegraphic signals), resulting in a massive expansion of public interest in radio.

Radio expanded rapidly during World War I. At the close of the war as many as a dozen companies in the United States were manufacturing radio transmitters and receivers, many of those sold on contract for military use. At first, the Marconi companies owned the patents on radio broadcasting and had subsidiaries in many countries, including the United States. Manufacturers and operators were required to obtain licensing and pay fees to the Marconi Company. General Electric, in part at the instigation of the U.S. Navy, bought the American Marconi Company and acquired its patents. In order to raise the necessary funds for the purchase, General Electric formed Radio Corporation of America, whose shares were bought by Westinghouse Corporation, American Telephone and Telegraph, United Fruit, and a number of other corporations. The plan was for AT&T's Western Electric subsidiary to build the transmitting equipment, while GE and Westinghouse focused on receivers.

David Sarnoff, who had been a manager for Marconi American, became general manager of RCA. In 1916, Sarnoff suggested the development of a "radio music box," but the corporate directors failed to act. Meanwhile, Frank Conrad, a Westinghouse engineer and an amateur radio operator, began transmitting phonograph music over his personal transmitter in Pittsburgh. It attracted substantial local attention. A local department store began selling an inexpensive radio receiver. Westinghouse then decided to build a more powerful radio transmitter and opened perhaps the first commercial radio station, KDKA. Almost concurrently, the Detroit *Evening News* began commercial broadcasts with music and news bulletins. Radio stations founded by Westinghouse, RCA, AT&T, and independents proliferated in 1920 and 1921. In the latter year AT&T established the first radio network. Numerous stations and networks opened in the next few years. Congress attempted to provide some order and direction by establishing the Federal Radio Commission in 1927. That structure broadened into the Federal Communications Commission in 1934.

TELEVISION: RADIO WITH PICTURES

The excitement and expansion of radio after World War I contributed the development of sound motion pictures in 1923 (another contribution by Lee De Forest), and to research on the transmission of pictures by radio waves. Television, or radio with pictures, emerged out of radio with the invention in 1923 of an iconoscope camera by Vladimir Zworykin, a Russian-born physicist and immigrant to the United States. In 1927 the transmission of televised pictures with sound had been achieved, and in 1928 the National Broadcasting Company began work on an experimental television transmitter, which began operations in 1931. Regular programming began in 1939 with a speech by Franklin D. Roosevelt opening the New York World's Fair.

The Federal Communications Commission authorized the first two commercial television stations (using VHF) in New York in July 1941. World War II interrupted expansion of the fledgling industry. In 1945 the FCC set aside a group of radio frequencies to be used for television transmission. Except for Mutual Broadcasting, three of the four major radio networks—NBC, CBS, and ABC—turned to television as adjuncts of their operations. Those companies, with the newly formed DuMont Television Network, subscribed to all channels available for television broadcast. New licenses were frozen until 1954 when the FCC authorized the use of UHF (Ultra High Frequency) channels for television broadcast.

The industry exploded. Broadcasting at the time was in black and white. Sets (receivers) were manufactured primarily by General Electric, RCA, Zenith, Curtis Mathes, Wells-Gardner Electronics, GTE Sylvania, Magnavox, Motorola, Philco, and a dozen other companies.

Commercial television became the hallmark of affluent Americans, for the most part, because they had the personal wealth and the option to channel spending into what was basically entertainment. In 1955 33.2 million, or 67 percent, of American homes had television sets; some homes even had two sets.

Color television was introduced in the mid-1950s. The United States was the major exporter of color and black-and-white television sets for a number of years. In 1964 American companies were manufacturing more than one million color television sets annually, and, as in the case of automobiles, consumed most of the world's product. Japanese companies manufactured only several thousand color sets in 1964, while European production was only beginning in earnest. The United States adopted what became known as the National Television System Committee (NTSC) standards for the manufacture of television sets. Europe, however (with some exceptions), because it began mass production after the United States using more advanced technology, adopted higher resolution (and more costly) technology for television standards generally referred to as PAL (German and European) or SECAM (French and Russian) standards.

What is significant about the global dimensions of the television industry is that from the United States' position of being almost the exclusive exporter of television sets in 1964, by 1977 it had lost almost half the market share to Japan. Indeed, in 1977 the United States imported 37 percent (two million) of its color television sets from Japan for domestic consumption. Japan, which had exported no color televisions in 1964, exported 42 percent of the world's supply in 1977.

As American auto manufacturers had anticipated that devaluation of the dollar would curtail the importation of Japanese automobiles, so television producers expected the same with television imports. Both, again, were disappointed. Japanese imports continued to rise. Japanese producers met the challenge of devaluation by improving the design and the reliability of its products. Integrated circuits replaced tubes and other electrical components. Japanese sets used variously 400 to 500 electrical components compared to American sets using an average of 600 components. Because American sets were traditionally marketed through small, independent retail establishments (involving higher distribution costs), Japanese marketing turned to large discount and department store chains for mass marketing, just at the time that such establishments were replacing the older, smaller, and more expensive distribution outlets traditionally used by American manufacturers. By 1977, the number of American television manufacturers had dropped from more than two dozen in 1960 to only five.

As they had in the automotive industry, television industry leaders attempted to meet the competition by largely cosmetic and inexpensive adjustments, such as redesigning the instrument and using different colors and cabinets or shells. American manufacturers sought relief from Congress and in the courts from unfair competition. Producers also began to move their production to lower-cost labor areas. Zenith opened factories in Mexico and Taiwan, and RCA went to Mexico. Japanese manufacturers countered the increased restrictions and restraints on imports being imposed by Congress. They solved the fundamental problem of transportation costs involved in manufacturing in Japan and selling in the United States by moving the production of television sets to the United States. Despite the fact that the United States levied a 15 percent tariff duty on picture tubes imported from Japan for assembly in the United States and virtually forced Japanese producers in the United States to purchase more expensive American picture tubes, Japanese plants were able to lower per-unit costs and improve reliability.

Sony began the production of color television sets in San Diego, California, in 1972; Matsushita in Franklin Park, Illinois, in 1974; and Sanyo in Forrest City, Arkansas, in 1976. American labor began turning out Japanese television sets bound for American markets—satisfying, in part at least, complaints by American labor leaders of unfair competition for foreign competitors. In 1978, Mitsubishi began production at Los Angeles and Toshiba in Lebanon, Tennessee. Sharp opened a factory in Memphis in 1979, and Hitachi established a plant in Los Angeles the same year. Although there were many explanations and reasons for the competitive successes of the Japanese, the primary reasons were more efficient production, better quality control, and effective market and distribution strategies.

Radio and television became intertwined with the inception of other audiovisual technologies. The Videocassette Recording (VCR) industry probably owed its inception to the audio (record) business more than it did to radio or television. Magnetic recording became well established during World War II primarily because of its use by the military. Recordings were made on instruments using spools of metal wire as the recording medium. During and after the war, the newly established plastics or polyester industry contributed by developing a flexible but reasonably strong plastic (acetate) magnetic tape. The tape proved more usable than the wire, and by 1950 wire recorders were being supplanted by tape recorders.

Although the recording of visual images on tape was theoretically possible, it proved to be a difficult technical problem. Videotape recordings required much broader frequency ranges than voice recordings. Mechanically that meant that a videotape had to travel at a much higher rate of speed than a voice tape. The problem was solved by Ampex Corporation engineers in California, who devised transverse (rather than longitudinal) recording and slowed the tape speed even more by using first two and then four recording heads, creating the quadruplex videotape recorder. Ampex began production in 1956 and soon licensed RCA to help build its recorders. Color was introduced in 1958.

Meanwhile, Japanese engineers began work on a similar transverse recording system, but were able to perfect the system by introducing helical scan recording, which proved to be less expensive and more reliable. A number of Japanese and American companies, including Sony, International Video Corporation (IVC), RCA, Panasonic, and Ampex, began manufacturing helical scan recorders using a half-inch- rather than a one-inch-wide tape, that proved more suitable for a general market. Each company, however, produced unique equipment and techniques such that recordings were not interchangeable. Finally, in 1971, the Electronics Industry Association of Japan (EIAJ) adopted standardized codes for production and both Japanese and American manufacturers began conforming to those standards. By that time, Japanese-made products dominated global trade in videocassette recorders (VCRs) and set the standards for the industry. The introduction of minicameras, cartridges, and cassettes gave Sony, in particular, leadership in the new home video industry, which came as an offspring of the larger commercial television industry.

Ampex, the American producer that first developed the transverse video recording system, also introduced a video disc recording system. That system provided a strong analogy to the existing audio record industry, and more significantly, eventually provided a new and vital ingredient for the computer industry that at first paralleled but did not interact with the developing audio/video industry.

A curious development in the television industry had to do with the reintroduction of the wire for "wireless" radio and television. Cable television seems to have developed in a number of independent locales in the late 1940s when several communities owning television sets but with no access to a suitable transmitter decided to build an antenna and then relay the signal by wire to their sets. This community antenna television system (CATV) grew rapidly between 1948 and 1952 when the FCC was declining to license new stations. CATVs could carry signals from the relatively few existing stations to more distant receivers. Cable TV ultimately created a whole new electronics industry and provided a pattern for interfacing telephone lines with television and computer communications. No sooner had cable service become a major part of the communications and television industry, but the cables became something other than wire. Fiber optics provided a new medium for the transfer of voices and data on streams of tiny laser pulses at the rate of millions of pulses per second on cables made of glass fibers.

Wireless communications in its purest form reached a new level of technological sophistication under the aegis of NASA-sponsored space experiments. In August 1960 NASA launched Echo I into orbit around the Earth. Echo I, a large balloon with an aluminized skin, was used to bounce radio signals from one point to another on Earth. Another passive relay satellite, Echo II, was placed in orbit in 1954. These experiments and the great communications revolution underway in the United States and elsewhere prompted AT&T (with NASA cooperation) to launch *Telstar I* in July 1962. *Telstar,* orbiting at a distance of approximately 100 miles about the Earth, received radio signals, amplified them, and retransmitted them back to receivers on the ground. That same year RCA launched a similar *Relay I* active communications satellite. Those satellites marked the real beginning of real-time global communications—but there were problems.

The low-Earth orbits of the satellites provided only periodic and limited use by any particular transmitter or receiver because of its 17,000 mile per hour speed around the globe. NASA solved that problem with the launch of a Hughes Aircraft–constructed geosynchronous communications satellite *Syncom I* in 1962. Placing a satellite in geosynchronous orbit meant that the satellite's orbit matched the Earth's rotation such that it could continuously receive and send signals from the same point on Earth twenty-four hours a day. That first satellite, however, suffered a mechanical failure and *Syncom II* was placed in orbit in 1963, followed by *Syncom III* in 1964. *Syncom III* perhaps demonstrated the new global synergy, and the rising interdependence of the Japanese and American economies by providing a real-time broadcast of the Tokyo Olympic games in the United States. Communications satellites, more so than any other medium, demonstrated the cohesion, the integrity, and the interdependence of the developing global community.

Global communications were facilitated by the organization of a congressionally created Communications Satellite Corporation (Comsat) in 1962. Its responsibility was to develop communications satellites for commercial use. AT&T invested in one-half of the Comsat stock, with the understanding that over the years it would (and did) divest itself of that stock, leaving Comsat as an independent corporation. Concurrently, the International Telecommunications Union associated with the United Nations sponsored the organization of the International Telecommunications Satellite Consortium or Intelsat. Comsat and Intelsat in turn funded the construction and launch of communications satellites under NASA management. NASA launched the first Intelsat communications satellite on April 6, 1965. Since that time, relying heavily upon the services of NASA's new space shuttle, which first flew in April 1981, communications satellites have been placed in orbit that can provide communications access between virtually any two points on Earth. AT&T (Comstar), Western Union (Westar), and RCA (Satcom) established global communications networks using their satellite relay stations.

Although the United States lost global market share in automotives, television, and in some of the electronics industries, the United States established itself as the undisputed leader in global communications and in the aerospace industries. Part of the explanation for the failure of the United States to compete more effectively in some of the established industries such as automotives and television may have been that the leading edge of American industrial development had turned into new channels of technology. Global communications, aerospace industries, medicine, and computers, juxtaposed with soft drinks and fast foods, helped establish the new reality of American business abroad during the last quarter of the twentieth century.

To a certain extent Americans began to act upon their own advice and counsel. It was becoming clear by the close of the decade of the 1970s that global competition was the new reality. The President's Commission on Industrial Competitiveness recommended, among other things, that American business take a new look at the opportunities of world trade and the new competitors we faced. Business should raise investment in productive assets and in the workforce. Americans must adopt a more flexible attitude toward changing markets and technologies. Labor and management must work together to strengthen the competitive performance of their firms. Competitiveness had to become a national priority. Business and government should work together to protect technology and encourage commercialization. Monetary policy and tax laws should provide inducements for capital investment. The federal government should conduct trade negotiations to improve the free flow and fairness of world trade.

The commission members concluded the following:

> The goal is clear and within reach. . . . We must perform up to our potential. Americans enjoy tackling a new problem. One lies before us now. To meet the challenge of competitiveness, we require only a new vision and a new resolve. We must acknowledge the reality of a new global economy—an economic era that has come quietly, without fanfare. And just as we explored a vast and unknown American frontier, we must chart a course into this new territory and claim it for the generations to come.

Chapter 8

BUSINESS: NOT AS USUAL

For most Americans a global economy seemed to be more a thing of the imagination than a reality in the early 1980s. The world was still divided between the communist and capitalist camps, and there was relatively little economic interchange between the two. The Soviet Union and China, in the communist camp, comprised almost one-half of the world's land mass and more than one-half of its peoples. There seemed to be little evidence that detente or cooperation could be achieved between the East and the West.

Too often, war seemed imminent. The United States strengthened its defenses. President Ronald Reagan strengthened the nation's military capabilities and introduced "Star Wars" technology to military preparations, hoping to be able to detect enemy missile attacks from observation satellites and to develop the ability to destroy attacking missiles in space before they entered the atmosphere. American expenditures for defense rose steadily from $240 billion in 1984 to $274 billion in 1987. Federal budget deficits and American trade imbalances worsened. The nation became embroiled in a new round of financial crises.

Employment in many manufacturing industries including iron and steel declined steadily. American steel production dropped from 130 million tons in 1970 to 88 million in 1985. In that year, for the first time in a century, the United States imported more industrial products, including automobiles and machinery, than it exported. Agricultural exports, which had risen steadily the previous decade, stabilized in the 1980s. Imports continued to rise. The United States achieved a $150 billion trade deficit in 1985, and became, for the first time in seventy years, a debtor nation.

Government policies designed to cope with the mounting financial problems often seemed counterproductive. Tax and spending reductions, deregulation, free trade, and tight monetary policies seemed to promote only rising unemployment and bigger trade deficits. But there were signs of progress. The inflationary spiral of the 1970s was checked. Surging petroleum prices began a retreat. By 1986, due to conservation measures in the United States and stepped-up exploration and production, world crude prices had collapsed from $32 per barrel to $12.50. Paradoxically, the reduction created a new round of financial instability.

Petroleum-producing and exporting areas and states, whose economies had become dependent on $32 per barrel oil, suffered a two-thirds decline in revenues. Recession struck the oil-producing areas of the United States, primarily the Southwest and Alaska. On a national scale, banks whose business was geared to petroleum (and most were to some extent) began to suffer losses as lenders were unable to meet their debt obligations. Many American banks had heavy loan investments in developing nations, much of that related to oil exploration and extraction. Mexico owed U.S. and international banks almost $100 billion, much of that secured by $32 per barrel oil — or the prospects of obtaining oil at that price. Geologists located almost 72 billion barrels of petroleum reserves in Mexico during the 1970s. Commercial U.S. banks such as Citicorp, Bank of America, and Manufacturers Hanover, as well as the World Bank and federal lending agencies provided funds for exploration and commercial development in Mexico, Brazil, Argentina, and many other nations.

The collapse in petroleum prices, coupled with rising unemployment in heavy industry, triggered declining real estate and property values in the United States. Property values began a sharp decline in many areas as in the "Rust Belt" where heavy industry was declining and in the Southwest and West where petroleum had become a mainstay of the economy. Banks, savings and loan institutions, and federal financial agencies became embroiled in a round of business failures and defaults.

Whereas fewer than ten banks on average failed in the United States in all the years between 1943 and 1981, failures and consolidations reached a rising crescendo in the 1980s. One hundred and thirty-eight banks failed in 1986; 184 in 1987. On October 19, 1987, the stock market, which had generally pursued an erratic but upward course for several decades, dropped 508 points in the day's trading, followed by a 77-point and a 156-point drop several days later. It seemed reminiscent of the October 1929 stock market crash that brought about the onset of the Great Depression.

Happily, there was no real comparison between the 1929 and 1987 drops. The 1987 drop came on the heels of a sharply rising market that fell to the negative persuasions of a renewed threat of inflation, growing trade deficits, lower corporate profits, and (something new) program trading driven by automated computer systems. What was significant about the financial problems of the 1980s is that the United States seemed to weather the problems quite well. The Federal Depositors Insurance Corporation (FDIC), which did not exist in 1929, prevented widespread loss from bank failures. The Resolution Trust Corporation (RTC) assumed the management of properties acquired from failed banks and provided, over time, for an orderly liquidation of assets. Financial crises and looming international defaults as with Mexico were avoided when World Bank, IMF, and the commercial banks affected worked out an accord with Mexico providing for new loans and long-term debt management coupled with financial reforms. In retrospect, the country seemed to handle its financial crisis extremely well.

While the American people were preoccupied with "Star Wars" and heightening tensions of the Cold War, and with the decline in energy costs and resultant bank failures, there were some fundamental but less obvious changes occurring in the domestic economy. In the decade of the 1980s, the American economy became considerably less domestic and more global. It also became less dependent upon heavy industry and more dependent upon high technology and services. A proliferation of multinational corporations in the 1980s created a stronger trade and financial interface among Western nations.

THE MULTINATIONAL CORPORATION

Multinational corporations (MNC) are businesses that do business in many countries. Classical examples of multinational corporations include the Dutch East India Company that set the pattern for European commercial expansion in the eighteenth and nineteenth centuries, or the British East India Company that received a monopoly on the sale of tea in the American colonies from the British Crown. The infamous Tea Act resulted in the Boston Tea Party. United Fruit dominated Central American business before 1900. Standard Oil, U.S. Rubber, Alcoa Aluminum, Goodyear Corporation, B. F. Goodrich, Western Electric, International Telephone and Telegraph, Eastman Kodak, and Coca-Cola were among the hundreds of American firms doing a global business through foreign-based subsidiaries at the turn of the century.

World War I, the Great Depression, and World War II considerably slowed American overseas business activities and investment. The Marshall Plan, European recovery, and the international infrastructure created by American foreign assistance programs and the World Bank stimulated a great increase in foreign investment by American firms after 1945. Unlike in earlier times much of the new post-1945 investment involved joint ventures, host country stock holders, and merger with or the purchase of foreign firms. Thus, the modern multinational corporation was more than simply an American business doing business in a foreign country (or conversely a foreign business operating in the United States). Rather the modern multinational increasingly represented a fusion of international interests and investment. Whether based in England, the United States, Japan, or elsewhere, the multinational tended to draw 25 percent or more of its income from outside its home country. The modern multinational ceased being essentially a colonial enterprise operating for the good of the mother country and instead developed true international, bilateral interests.

In that capacity, for a time, the multinational became somewhat suspect in the United States. George Orwell's science fiction epic *1984*, for example, intimated that a multinational corporation might become so big and powerful that it could supplant the state and traditional government. Could the corporation rather than government become the principal organizing structure of human society? There were some sticky and interesting constitutional and human rights issues involved in such a question. But in reality there seemed to be no evidence whatsoever that an "Orwellian" society could develop from the multinational scene. Rather, the multinational corporation drew heavily from organized government for support. Treaties, trade agreements, and national policy often reflected the international interests of the corporation. Thus, the MNC provided an incentive for international cooperation and exchange and stimulated the development of a global community.

American business investment abroad rose from $32 billion in 1960 to $1.7 trillion by 1987. American petroleum operations became truly international, penetrating into previously forbidden areas in Asia and the Middle East. American petroleum and petrochemical interests led American overseas expansion, spurred on by the almost desperate search for fuel and energy after the OPEC embargo. Union Carbide provides a good example of how an American petrochemical company became a true multinational corporation after World War II.

Union Carbide Corporation had its origins with the Virginia incorporation of Union Carbide Company, a producer of calcium carbide, in 1898. In 1917, Union Carbide, Linde Air Products (an Ohio manufacturer of oxyacetylene welding gas), National Carbon Company (a New York company that manufactured electrodes and arc lamps), and Presto-O-Lite (a New York–based manufacturer of calcium carbide used for portable lamps) were joined as Union Carbide and Carbon Corporation. Union Carbide emerged from World War II with fifteen virtually independent and autonomous divisions. After 1963, Union Carbide began a rigorous reorganization program that involved divesting itself of some operations and adding others to strengthen its profits and centralized management. Major operating divisions included battery products, carbon products, electronics, hydrocarbons, films, medical products, metals, nuclear materials, silicones, and solvents. A major strategy followed in its overseas expansion was to include host-country participation in the ownership of its subsidiaries. Regional divisions established at various points on the globe provided management oversight for operating subsidiaries within the region.

A sense of Union Carbide's global operations, its management, and host-country participation is indicated by the following table of Union Carbide's regional divisions. The percentage figure in parenthesis indicates Union Carbide's percent of ownership—the remainder being host country or regional ownership. In 1984, Union Carbide India's plant in Bhopal released a cloud of poisonous gas that killed more than 2000 people. Union Carbide offered to create a trust fund of $230 million to provide compensation to the victims and more than a decade of litigation followed.

TABLE 8–1
Union Carbide, Global Operations: 1982

REGIONAL DIVISION

UNION CARBIDE AFRICA AND MIDDLE EAST, INC.

Country	Subsidiary	Percent Owned by Union Carbide
Egypt	Union Carbide Egypt S.A.E.	75%
Ghana	Union Carbide Ghana Limited	66.7%
Ivory Coast	Cote Union Carbide Cote d'Ivoire	100%
Kenya	Union Carbide Kenya Limited	65%
Nigeria	Union Carbide Nigeria Limited	60%
Saudi Arabia	Carbide Hashim Industrial Gases	25%
Sudan	Union Carbide Sudan Limited	84%

UNION CARBIDE CANADA LIMITED

Canada	Union Carbide Canada Limited	74.72%

UNION CARBIDE EASTERN, INC.

Australia	Chemos Industries Pty. Limited	60.02%
	Union Carbide Australia Limited	60.02%
Hong Kong	Sonea Industries Limited	100%
	Union Carbide Asia Limited	100%
India	Union Carbide India Limited	50.9%
Indonesia	P.T. Agrocarb Indonesia	70.7%
	P.T. Union Carbide Indonesia	100%
Japan	Nippon Unicar Company Limited	50%
	Union Showa K.K.	50%
	Sony-Eveready, Inc.	50%
	Union Carbide Services Eastern	100%
Korea	Union Gas Company Limited	86.15%
Malaysia	Union Carbide Malaysia Sdn. Bhd.	80%
	Union Polymers Sdn. Bhd.	60%
New Zealand	Union Carbide New Zealand Limited	60.02%
Philippines	Union Carbide Philippines, Inc.	100%
Sri Lanka	Union Carbide Ceylon Limited	60%
Singapore	Metals and Ores Pte. Limited	100%
	Union Carbide Singapore Pte. Ltd.	100%
Thailand	Union Carbide Thailand Limited	100%

TABLE 8–1 (CONTINUED)

Union Carbide, Global Operations: 1982

REGIONAL DIVISION

UNION CARBIDE EUROPE, INC.

Country	Subsidiary	Percent Owned by Union Carbide
Belgium	Union Carbide Benelux N.V.	100%
	Indugas N.V.	50%
France	La Littorale S.A.	99.95%
	Union Carbide France S.A.	100%
	Viscora S.A.	50%
West Germany	Ucar Battenen G.m.b.H.	100%
	Union Carbide Deutschland G.m.b.H.	100%
	Union Carbide Industriegase G.m.b.H.	100%
Greece	Union Carbide Hellas Industrial	100%
Italy	Elettrografite Meridionale S.p.A.	100%
	Uniliq S.p.A.	100%
	Union Carbide Italia S.p.A.	100%
Spain	Argon, S.A.	50%
	Union Carbide Iberica, S.A.	100%
	Union Carbide Navarra, S.A.	100%
Sweden	Unifos Kemi AB	50%
	Union Carbide Norden AB	100%
Switzerland	Union Carbide Europe S.A.	100%
United Kingdom	Union Carbide U.K. Limited	100%
	Viskase Limited	50%

UNION CARBIDE PAN AMERICA, INC.

Argentina	Union Carbide Argentina, S.A.I.C.S.	99.99%
Brazil	Eletro Manganes Lida	55%
	Tungstento do Brasil Minerios et Metais Lida	55%
	S.A. White Martins	50.14%
	S.A. White Martins Nordeste	50.14%
	Union Carbide do Brasil Lida	100%
Colombia	Union Carbide Colombia, S.A.	100%
Costa Rica	Union Carbide Centro Americana, S.A.	100%
Ecuador	Union Carbide Ecuador, C.A.	100%
Mexico	Union Carbide Mexicana, S.A. de C.V.	45.70%
Venezuela	Union Carbide de Venezuela, C.A.	100%

TABLE 8–1 (CONTINUED)
Union Carbide, Global Operations: 1982

REGIONAL DIVISION

UNION CARBIDE PUERTO RICO, INC.

Country	Subsidiary	Percent Owned by Union Carbide
Puerto Rico	Union Carbide Caribe, Inc.	100%
	Union Carbide Films-Packaging, Inc.	100%
	Union Carbide Grafito, Inc.	100%

UNION CARBIDE SOUTHERN AFRICA, INC.

Republic of South Africa		
	Elektrode Maatskappy Van Suid Afrika (Eiendoms) Beperk	50%
	Tubatse Ferrochrome (Proprietary)	49%
	Ucar Chrome Company (S.A.) Prop. Ltd.	100%
	Ucar Minerals Corporation	100%
Zimbabwe (unconsolidated subsidiaries)		
	Zimbabwe Mining and Smelting Company (Private) Limited	100%
	Union Carbide Zimbabwe (Private) Ltd.	100%

Among the interesting facets of Union Carbide's global operations are the regional administrative divisions. The company divided the world into North Africa and Middle East; South Africa; the East (Japan and the Pacific Rim); Europe; and Pan America. Nations notably absent from the regions associated with Union Carbide are China and the Soviet Union. The regional administrative system adopted by Union Carbide reflects the federated economic regions that were developing around the globe. If one adds North America (Canada, the United States, and Mexico joined by NAFTA agreements in 1993), China, and Russia and the Commonwealth of Independent States to Union Carbide's regional divisions, the outline of the developing federated global economy begins to appear.

By the 1980s the global economy was beginning to emerge as a loose trading association among regionally federated but essentially autonomous national economies. The expansion of the multinational corporation in the 1970s and 1980s provided some of the interface between the regional economies. The multinational corporation was by no means a uniquely American institution.

Foreign investment in the United States grew from about $8 billion in 1950 to $1.54 trillion in 1987. In the 1970s particularly, devaluation attracted heavy foreign investment in the United States. Japanese and Saudi Arabian investors joined the ranks of the traditional British, West German, French, and Dutch investors. Japanese investment in the United States rose from $0.2 billion in 1970 to more than $33 billion by 1987. Honda, Toyota, and Subaru opened automotive plants in the United States. By the 1990s Honda had more employees outside Japan than within. Sony began making color television sets in Southern California. Masushita bought Motorola's television division and began manufacturing Panasonic sets in America. Japanese investors bought shopping centers, hotels, office buildings, and race tracks. Japan became the world's leading banker. The world's ten largest banks in 1987 were Japanese owned. Citibank of New York, America's largest bank, ranked twenty-eighth among world banks. Seventeen of the world's twenty-five strongest banks were Japanese, and the remaining eight were West German, British, French, or Swiss owned.

That heavy foreign investment slowed America's trade imbalance and established or strengthened business relationships between the United States and the investor nations. British investors bought American newspapers and magazines. Baskin-Robbins, an American ice cream and sandwich franchise, became a part of Allied Brewing of Great Britain. Bayer of Germany purchased Miles Laboratories. Nestle acquired the American foods giant, Libby, McNeil & Libby. Individuals throughout the world acquired interests in American companies through independent and mutual-fund stock purchases. Conversely, American investment houses offered shares in foreign companies independently or in any portfolio format the investor might desire.

The Americanization of the global economy and the development of an infrastructure for the conduct of business, travel, and trade continued with the expansion of American hotel chains such as the Hilton, Sheraton, and Holiday Inns throughout the world— excluding for a time China and the Soviet Union. The inauguration of French-built Concorde supersonic service between the United States and London in 1976 and between the United States and Paris in 1978 put commuter time between the three countries at three and one-half hours. Regular jet service and passenger miles flown between the United States, Europe, and Japan and Southeast Asia expanded massively in the 1980s, as did cruise ship passenger service.

America's McDonald's restaurants expanded rapidly in the 1980s and
1990s, opening restaurants in the greater and lesser cities of the world
from Moscow, Budapest, Vienna, and Paris to Beijing.

(Reuters/Bettmann Newsphotos)

McDonald's hamburger franchise business became international
in the 1980s. McDonald's, the byword for American fast foods, was
created in 1954 by Ray Kroc, a paper cup and milkshake machine
salesman, when he was 52 years old. Impressed with a San Bernar-
dino, California, hamburger drive-in, Kroc convinced the McDonald
brothers to allow him to franchise operations based on their model.
The original agreement provided that he would receive $950 for
each franchise opened and 1.4 percent of the operation's gross receipts, while the McDonalds received 0.5 percent of gross receipts.
Later, Kroc bought the McDonald interest out for $2.7 million and
offered McDonald's stock to the public. By 1986 there were 9410
McDonald's restaurants in operation in the United States and the
foreign operations were just beginning. By the close of the decade
there were few cities in Europe without a McDonald's franchise, and
operations were beginning in Japan and Southeast Asia. McDonald's
franchise operations adapted readily to foreign operations because
they involved host-country ownership and management.

Coca-Cola, which began in Atlanta, Georgia, became the most widely consumed beverage in the world. Coca-Cola established its first foreign operations in Canada about 1900. Introduced to Europe and Asia by American GIs during World War II, Coca-Cola never really left. By 1970 more than one-half of the Coca-Cola consumed was sold outside of the United States. Coca-Cola expansion rested heavily on the concept of locally owned and operated bottling plants and distributors. Employees were overwhelmingly citizens of the host countries. Coca-Cola described its multinational policy as a "partnership in industry."

In the early 1980s Coca-Cola began diversifying into other businesses, including the acquisition of Columbia Pictures Entertainment. That, according to its CEO, Roberto Goizueta, diverted the company from its main business—selling soft drinks around the world. As one Coca-Cola executive expressed, "When I think of Indonesia, a country on the Equator, with 180 million people, a median age of eighteen, and a Moslem ban on alcohol, I feel I know what heaven looks like." Coca-Cola went to Indonesia, Japan, and China. Coca-Cola was one of only two American companies permitted by Japan to operate a wholly American-owned subsidiary there. The other company was IBM. China, which had been closed to Coca-Cola since the chairmanship of Mao Tse-tung, readmitted Coca-Cola for public sale in 1979. At that time, China had a billion people who consumed an average of *one* soft drink a year.

"When the Berlin Wall collapsed in 1990, the company rushed into East Germany, where a consumer survey showed 99 percent of the people still knew the name Coca-Cola, even though the product had not been for sale there since World War II." When Coca-Cola trucks first entered Warsaw, Poland, crowds cheered. Coca-Cola's policy of "think globally, act locally" reflected not just Coca-Cola, but a developing pattern of response by American business to the challenge of global competition. Coca-Cola became "seen and accepted as a universal concomitant of Americanism around the world." That may also have caused Chairman Mao Tse-tung to expressly forbid the sale of Coca-Cola and Pepsi in China.

Pepsi-Cola followed closely on Coca-Cola's overseas expansion. Pepsi opened its first plant in Canada in 1934, followed by plants in Cuba and the Dominican Republic. Pepsi's international efforts subsided until after World War II, when in 1957, Donald M. Kendall became president of Pepsi-Cola International. Kendall, the son of a Washington state dairy farmer who was twice awarded the Distin-

In every language Coca-Cola became a recognized and widely consumed American product and a factor in the "Americanization of the Global Economy."

(UPI/Corbis-Bettmann)

guished Flying Cross as a Navy pilot during World War II, began work with Pepsi-Cola in 1947 selling fountain syrup in New York City. During his first three years as head of Pepsi's international operations, Kendall opened a new locally owned and operated overseas bottling plant every 11.5 days. In the 1960s Pepsi teamed with Schweppes in England, Perrier in France, and Heineken in the Netherlands to expand European sales. In 1966 Pepsi opened plants in Belgium and Austria. While both Coca-Cola and Pepsi contributed to the Americanization of the global economy, both, particularly in the 1980s and following, restructured their own operations to better fit the global environment.

The United States contributed mightily to the Americanization of the global environment after World War II by introducing the computer as a device "that could actually be placed within the grasp of ordinary men and women the world over." Subsequently, efforts by American firms to meet the global competition that resulted from the computer revolution forced a restructuring of American business methods and management. The technology that created computers, radio, and television began to merge and build the sinews that knit together more tightly the new global community. Multinationals, hotels, fast foods, soft drinks, amusement parks, airlines, and computers provided yet another global business interface for the 1980s and beyond.

THE COMPUTER REVOLUTION

The conception of the modern computer is usually attributed to Charles Babbage, a mathematician who in 1833 designed a mechanical analytical engine driven by steam that could perform mathematical and algebraic computations. It was never built, but it provided inspiration to others such as Charles Sanders Peirce, an American logician who decided in the 1880s that an electrical switching circuit could be used to build a calculating machine. The first model of an electric logic machine was built in 1936 by Benjamin Burak. The machine had limited use, but may have inspired an IBM decision to fund the development of an electromechanical calculating machine by Howard Aiken, a Harvard professor. Aiken completed his "electronic brain," called the Mark 1, in 1944. While Aiken was working on Mark 1, John Atanasoff, a professor of mathematics and physics at Iowa State College designed a computer that used vacuum tubes rather than electrical relays. Although Atanasoff built a prototype, the device never became operational. It did, however, make the Mark 1's electrical relay systems obsolete even before the machine was completed. Inspired by Atanasoff's work, John Mauchly and J. Presper Eckert at the Moore School of Engineering in Philadelphia designed and began building a machine called ENIAC that used only vacuum tubes. They received some assistance from John Von Neumann who tilted their work away from pure calculations to a machine that could perform both arithmetic and logical operations.

While it was being built, ENIAC was put to work performing calculations for the Los Alamos laboratories. ENIAC was completed in 1946, setting the standard for high-performance calculations. Sperry Univac (formerly Remington Typewriter Company and later Sperry Rand) began manufacturing the Univac computer. For a time Univac became synonymous with "computer." Mauchly and Eckert failed to sustain their patents against challenges from IBM, supported by John Atanasoff, and the world of mainframe computing opened to competitors. Although IBM came to dominate the business within a few years, Control Data Corporation, Honeywell, Burroughs, General Electric, RCA, and NCR all competed.

Incorporated in 1911 as the Computing-Tabulating-Recording Company, the name was changed in 1924 to International Business Machines Corporation following acquisitions and mergers. IBM entered the computer business in 1951, and at the end of the decade began to standardize computers and operations with the introduction of its "360" line of computers. Mainframe computers were expensive and often leased rather than purchased. They were primarily used by research scientists, the military, and large businesses.

The great innovation that transformed the computer industry from the mainframe multimillion dollar machine staffed by dozens of engineers and technicians into a personal computer usable by ordinary men and women was the development of a transistor to replace the vacuum tube. The transistor in turn led to the development of the integrated circuit. The integrated circuit allowed for the construction of compact, fairly sophisticated, and relatively inexpensive personal computers. As often the case, the development of the transistor (microchip) and the integrated circuit had circuitous origins.

William Shockley and a group of Bell Laboratory research associates developed a working but unrefined transistor in 1948. Shockley left Bell Laboratories and organized Shockley Semiconductor Laboratories in Santa Clara Valley near San Francisco in 1954 for work on the development of transistors. Eight of his employees left him in 1957 to organize Fairchild Semiconductor, in competition with Shockley. Close at hand, another pioneer electronics firm organized in 1939 in a Palo Alto garage with a $538 capital investment by William Hewlett and David Packard began the manufacture of electronic oscillators.

In Texas in 1951, Geophysical Services Incorporated, which had begun in 1930 as a seismographic oil exploration company and then became involved in electronic research projects for the military during World War II, reorganized as Texas Instruments. Texas Instruments soon merged with International Rubber Company and received development contracts for work on the transistor from Bell Laboratories. In 1954 Texas Instruments' Gordon Teal developed a silicone transistor that was far superior to the existing transistors. Subsequently, Jack Kilby, also with Texas Instruments, perfected a system to manufacture electronic circuits on semiconductor chips (silicone transistors) and filed for patents on his integrated circuit design in 1959. Almost concurrently, Robert Noyce with Fairchild

Semiconductors improved upon the integrated circuit with one-piece imbedded circuit design. Following lawsuits filed by TI, companies producing integrated circuit boards required licenses from both Fairchild and Texas Instruments. Noyce left Fairchild and organized Intel Development Corporation. In 1969, Intel received a large contract from a Japanese calculator company to produce microchips for its instruments. The semiconductor and integrated circuit transformed the electronics industry after 1960. Texas Instruments' sales rose an average of 30 percent each year between 1954 and 1974. Texas Instruments broadened its product line to include semiconductors, calculators, integrated circuits, electronic data-processing equipment (computers), and aircraft control and guidance systems. Sales rose from $230 million in 1960 to $1.6 billion by 1975.

Another electronics venture began in Albuquerque, New Mexico, in 1968, when Ed Roberts, Forest Mims, and several Air Force officers began manufacturing radio transmitters for model airplanes and selling them through mail order. The company was called Micro Instrumentation Telemetry Systems (MITS). Roberts bought his partners out in 1969 and began producing programmable calculators to sell in kit form. Roberts lost heavily in the growing market for hand-held calculators, but in 1974 he introduced a computer kit designed for household use employing a microchip developed by Intel called the 8080. The Altair computer sold for about $400, lower even than the cost of an 8080 chip. By buying in quantity, Roberts had secured chips at $75 each. It was, as a practical matter, the first computer really aimed for the mass public market.

The Altair sold exceptionally well. Roberts's MITS moved from a $400,000 debt to $250,000 in profits within a matter of weeks. But the Altair and most early machines lacked adequate memory storage and software or "machine language" for them to be effective for the ordinary person. Roberts solved that problem by having Paul Allen, a Honeywell employee, and Bill Gates, a freshman at Harvard University, design a BASIC program, that is, the numeric code system that directed the central processing unit (CPU) of the computer. Roberts then hired Allen as MITS software director. In 1975, Allen and Gates founded Microsoft Corporation, a manufacturer of computer software. Subsequently, Microsoft introduced MS-DOS, which became the foundation for computer language, and then Microsoft Windows, which became the management software for most personal computers. But for a short time, Altair set the standard for personal computers. In 1977 Roberts sold MITS and Altair subsequently disappeared from the computer lists. That same year Tandy Corporation (Radio Shack) and Apple Computer Company introduced personal computers.

Steven Jobs and Stephen Wozniak incorporated Apple Computer Company in 1977 and introduced the Apple II, a remarkable user-friendly computer with color graphics and optional software programs designed for personal and home use. The company went public in 1980, and by 1982 had sales exceeding $1 billion annually. The Lisa, MacIntosh, Mac Plus, and laser printers and a wide assortment of games and software gave Apple leadership in the computer industry for only a few years. By 1986, competition was beginning to make inroads on Apple's fortunes. In 1981, IBM, which had refrained from entering the personal computer market while protecting its mainframe industry, introduced the IBM PC, which used Microsoft's MS-DOS machine language. For most of the decade IBM set the standards for personal computers, dominating the domestic and world markets. By the 1990s, that dominance had begun to fade.

Compaq Computer Corporation, based in Houston, Texas, began to move ahead of other competitors in sales. Microchip producers faced rising competition from Asian and Japanese producers. American computer manufacturers began to turn their attention to overseas markets to develop overseas production facilities for microchips and computers. Hewlett-Packard, for example, established manufacturing plants, research centers, and administrative offices in more than one hundred countries. A Hewlett-Packard desktop laser printer sold 60 percent of the $13 billion global market in 1992. Compaq became the world's largest PC maker, followed by IBM, Apple, Packard Bell, and NEC Corporation. The American computer industry became a global, multinational, many-faceted business. By 1990, American computer manufacturers were selling more computers abroad than in the United States. In 1995 computer manufacturers shipped 60 million personal computers, 22.5 million of those to U.S. buyers and the remainder overseas. The world's business acquired a new dimension. Computers and communication systems began to rival automobiles, aircraft, energy, and weapons as major global industries. The computer created a new communications and business interface for the developing global community. The last decade of the twentieth century began with the world on the edge of dramatic changes.

Beginning in 1990, national governments began to adapt to the developing reality of a global community and a global economy. The communist government of the Soviet Union and its satellites collapsed. Russia began to become more fully integrated into the global economy and the world community. Nations took political steps toward supporting free trade and commerce among themselves through more intensive and substantive General Agreements on Tariffs and Trade. The European Common Market became the European Union, and the United States broadened its hemispheric cooperation with Canada and Mexico through the North American Free Trade Agreement (NAFTA). The global economy became more fully a cluster of federated regional economies in which traditional national interests were somewhat subordinated to regional interests. The old nation-state was being supplanted by a new global community, the national economies by a global economy, and the corporation no longer could be thought of by its country of origin. There were some signs of a "new world order" in the making.

Chapter 9

TOWARD A NEW WORLD ORDER

President George Bush prescribed a new world order to replace the almost half-century of Cold War that had divided the world. That order was already in the making. It began with the dissolution of the communist regime in the Soviet Union. It continued with the affirmation of the Economic Union in Europe. It developed further with the North American attempts at economic union represented by the North American Free Trade Agreement. It involved the settlement of the half-century dispute over the West Bank in Israel. It related to the greater tendency of China to open its borders to outside trade and commerce. It had to do with a rising sense of global stability, security, and order, and the implementation of multilateral global trade agreements. It had much to do with the end of the Union of Soviet Socialist Republics.

THE SOVIET COUNTERREVOLUTION

The dissolution of the communist regime in the Soviet Union and the end of the Cold War is one of the most remarkable political and economic events of modern times. It is as remarkable for the way it occurred as it is in the fact that it occurred at all. The Soviet Union simply imploded, quietly and almost benignly—in stark contrast to its revolutionary beginnings. Mikhail Sergeyevich Gorbachev, who became general-secretary of the Communist party in 1985 and president of the Union of Soviet Socialist Republics in 1988, stood in the center of this history. He was variously the pilot, the helmsman, or the unwitting passenger. As party secretary and president of the Soviet Union, Gorbachev assisted if not directed the transfer of power from the Communist party to popularly elected legislatures in the republics. In 1989, the Berlin Wall, dividing the communist and free worlds, opened. The communist government of East Germany collapsed and Germany was reunited. Poland, Hungary, and Czechoslovakia held free elections and established their independence from the Soviet Union. Gorbachev's policy of perestroika sought to return at least some elements of the economy to the private sector. Under his direction the Soviet Union sought to normalize relations with the United States and China. The Soviet Union agreed to arms controls, withdrew troops from Afghanistan, and at least passively supported the United States in its efforts to oust Iraq following that country's invasion of Kuwait. That inaction, if not support, marked a strong departure from the Cold War tradition of confrontation.

The Soviet economy suffered a collapse in 1991. It was a collapse presumably long in progress because of the continuing demands and costs of Cold War armaments and the low productivity of the communist, state-owned and state-directed economy. As hard times struck the Soviet Union, factions lined up in opposition to the government seeking a full return to the communist system on the one hand, or a complete break with the communist past and the institution of free-market capitalism on the other.

On Tuesday, August 20, 1991 (Monday the 19th in the United States), Soviet communist officials placed Gorbachev under house arrest and seized power as the State Committee for the State of Emergency. The committee included the head of the KGB, the Soviet security force; the Defense Minister, Interior Minister, the Vice President, and the Prime Minister. Vice President Gennady Yanayev declared himself acting president. The committee announced the seizure of power in order to "forestall a mortal danger that has come to loom large over our great motherland." The policies of reform, "seeking to ensure the country's dynamic development and the democratization of social life," had failed. "The chaotic, spontaneous slide towards a market provoked an explosion of egoism—regional, departmental, group and personal." The "centrifugal tendencies" were destroying the "integral national economic mechanism." While the committee pledged to "support private enterprise, granting it necessary opportunities for the development of production and ser-

President George Bush who sought "a new world order"—got it. He served as president of the United States during the most remarkable global changes in modern times. The Cold War ended and on December 8, 1991, the Union of Soviet Socialists Republics was peacefully disbanded.

(Reuters/Bettmann Newsphotos)

vices," the interim government also pledged to return to central authority and to reestablish the state.

"The whole world will be affected" by events in the Soviet Union, commented a South Korean official upon hearing about the ouster of Mikhail Gorbachev. New Zealand's Prime Minister Jim Bolger called the crisis in the Soviet Union "a major event which could significantly destablize the world economy and possibly even destablise it politically." A Russian ballet choreographer visiting in Hong Kong during the Moscow crisis was shocked and concerned at the political changes occurring in the Soviet Union, but he believed that it was impossible for the Soviet Union to turn back. "We are now building a free and open society."

China had mixed emotions. China's supreme leader, Deng Xiaoping, blamed the fall of socialism in Eastern Europe and the internal economic and political problems in the Soviet Union on Gorbachev's "misguided perestroika," but China had also appreciated the Sino-Soviet rapprochement made possible by Gorbachev's initiatives and visit to Beijing in May 1989, despite the fact that Gorbachev's visit contributed to the pro-democracy movement and a confrontation at Tiananmen Square. While Soviet power was a perceived threat to China, instability in the Soviet Union was also threatening.

But the Soviet people wanted change. Russia's president Boris Yeltsin climbed on a tank outside the Russian parliament in Moscow and called for the public to reject the restoration of the Soviet Union by the hard-liners. The coup lasted sixty hours. Supporters of reform restored Gorbachev to power. U.S. President George Bush announced that "democracy, freedom and reform have prevailed" in the Soviet Union and he predicted a strengthening of U.S.-Soviet relations and a "gigantic leap forward for democracy" in the Soviet Union. Gorbachev then resigned as the Communist party secretary and effectively ended the party's control over government. Russian President Boris Yeltsin subsequently banned the Communist party from Russia.

Russia and its associated republics entered a time of great trial and confusion, but a time notably marked by the prevalence of peace rather than by war and by the construction of the apparatus of a free market economy. Boris N. Yeltsin now became the champion of reform in Russia and in the republics of the former Soviet Union. He sought to further demolish the central government's control, to forge a federation of new republics, turn the economy to private enterprise, and demilitarize Russian industry.

On December 8, 1991, the Union of Soviet Socialist Republics was peacefully disbanded. Russia, Belarus, and the Ukraine, formerly members of the Soviet Union, united as the Commonwealth of Independent States (CIS), an association modeled on the European Community. Two weeks later they were joined by other former members of the Soviet Union, including Armenia, Azerbaijan, Kazakhstan, Kyrgystan, Moldova, Tajikistan, Turkmenistan, and Uzbekistan. Estonia, Latvia, and Lithuania remained independent republics. Georgia joined the CIS in 1994. The CIS sought to reconstruct the Soviet Union as a commonwealth of independent nation-states united into a common economic and mutual defense union. CIS member states retained a common currency and in theory they embraced a free market economy and common trade and immigration policies. Long-range strategic and nuclear weapons were to remain under the control of the Russian president and the army was reconstituted as the army of the Commonwealth.

The Soviet Union was gone. Gorbachev became a private citizen. Russia had seemingly completed one of the most radical and bloodless revolutions of all time. The Western world and the United States were astonished and eager to participate in the privatization of Russia and the Commonwealth republics. The U.S. Army began a phased withdrawal from Western Europe. McDonald's Corporation opened a restaurant in Moscow. The reality of a global economy pressed more closely.

CHINA AND THE GLOBAL ECONOMY

How would events in Russia affect China and its relations to the world? Having only the previous year crushed a reform march and demonstration in Beijing's Tiananmen Square, China seemed at first disposed to side strongly with the Soviet hard-liners. Beneath the hard exterior, however, lurked a China somewhat eager to reclaim its historic position in international trade and commerce. China's acquisition of Hong Kong, to occur in 1997, while clouded by other rhetoric, was part of that rising interest in outside commerce. The 1984 agreement with Great Britain stipulated that China agreed to preserve Hong Kong's economic and legal systems for at least another 50 years. Hong Kong had already become a vital link in China and Southeast Asia trade. Hong Kong imported some $72 billion in goods in the late 1980s and exported a larger amount. Hong Kong was the rising commercial hub of the Pacific Rim.

The constant mainland China threat/overture toward Taiwan and the national Chinese government also reflected to some small degree an interest in extending China toward the West. China, with less enthusiasm for democracy and capitalism and even more central control than the Soviet Union, was developing an interest in change. China adopted, then seemingly abandoned, a number of modernization programs after 1976. In 1979 China established full diplomatic relations and signed a limited trade agreement with the United States.

U.S. Secretary of Commerce Ron Brown (left) and the Peoples Republic of China Minister of Foreign Trade Wu Yi sign an agreement aimed at expanding trade and economic cooperation in 14 areas between the two countries during a ceremony in Beijing on August 29, 1994. Brown and a delegation of American businessmen and trade representatives died in an airplane crash on a mission to restore trade and commerce in war-torn Bosnia in 1996.

(AP/Wide World Photos)

After 1980 China increased its efforts to attract Western technology and investment.

The collapse of the Soviet Union seemed, after a time of uncertainty, to have stimulated further change and reform in China, at least to the extent of making market enterprises more acceptable, if not desirable. Western business and government leaders actively solicited China's business. China offered 1.2 billion people and the world's fastest-growing major economy. In 1992, McDonald's opened a "Golden Arches" restaurant in Beijing. Germany's Chancellor Helmut Kohl took a contingent of German businessmen through China and landed $4 billion in contracts for German companies. U.S. Commerce Secretary Ron Brown followed with an American business entourage, securing $6 billion in business for American companies. In 1994, Canada's Prime Minister Gauchos Chretien won $8.6 billion in contracts for Canadians. Foreign investors eagerly put their money into China. During 1994 foreign investors poured an average of $83 million daily into China.

China appeared to be joining the global economy, but in somewhat eratic fashion. In 1994, the government ordered the razing of the Beijing buildings surrounding the McDonald's restaurant. General Motors, Ford, Chrysler, and Toyota motor companies applied for licenses to open automotive assembly plants in China. The government made the assembly plant conditional upon the corporations establishing a parts manufacturing plant in China before they could be licensed for an assembly plant. Any assembly plants had to have majority control by Chinese stockholders. After a year of negotiations General Electric neared an agreement with Chinese authorities for the construction of two large power generating plants when the company was informed that a majority interest in the plants had to be in Chinese hands. State-owned Chinese enterprises loaned $600 million by Japanese, German, and Italian banks defaulted on their obligations. China's enforcement of Western patents and copyrights was notoriously lax. If capitalism had in fact arrived in China, it was being closely monitored and directed—or ignored—by the government. Beijing set quotas for the number of companies that could issue stock in any one year, the number of shares that could be issued, and the minimum price-earnings ratio at which a Chinese company's stock might be listed in foreign offerings.

It was not a free market economy, but compared to the past, China had become an open market. As one American business executive commented, "China is large enough to write its own rules."

In the 1990s, Russia and the Commonwealth of States, formerly the Soviet Union, and China, home of almost one-fourth of the world's peoples, were slowly and not always surely being annexed to the global economy. That condition began to alter the nature of the global economy. China and the Commonwealth of States comprised two very large and largely autonomous regional economic entities each of whom could place large bargaining chips on the tables of global commerce and trade. The admission of China and the Commonwealth of States to the global economic community provided new incentives to European, American, and Japanese governments and business to seek cooperation and compromise and to further consolidate their own national identities within a regional economic unit sufficient in size and strength to barter successfully with the Chinese and Russian units and with each other.

Although by no means the driving incentive to economic union, the emerging Chinese and Russian free market economies provided an additional stimulant to the creation of the Economic Union in Europe and to the organization of the North American Free Trade Association that brought Canada, the United States, and Mexico into at least the preliminary stages of what could one day be economic union.

THE EUROPEAN UNION

The Maastrict Treaty transforming the European Community into the European Union was ratified by the twelve member states in 1993. Internal trade barriers were virtually eliminated. Citizens of one country could pass freely throughout the Union. Austria elected to join the Union in 1994; Norway declined. The implementation of a common currency and a European army were delayed, but planned. Unrelated to the mechanics of union, but very related to the mechanics of trade and commerce, a tunnel (the Chunnel) linking Great Britain and France opened in 1995 and provided another integrating link. The European Union, long in development, effectively brought 500 million people into a powerful regional common market and economic association.

NAFTA

As in the case of the European Union, the origins and incentives behind the North American Free Trade Association (NAFTA) did not relate directly to the emerging China and Commonwealth of States regional economies. But the coalescence of those new market economies with the strengthening of European commercial bonds and the growing competition from Japan that exercised "price and market" leadership over the Pacific Rim economies prompted the United States to knit its trade associations in North America more tightly.

The real trigger to NAFTA was the end of the OPEC embargo and the subsequent collapse of crude petroleum prices. During the oil shortages, U.S. oil exploration and development companies, supported by government loans and commercial banks, invested large sums in Mexico funded largely on the premise of $32 per barrel crude. By the mid-1980s, Mexico had become deeply mired in debt. The United States, long a trading partner of Mexico, was sorely affected by Mexico's financial problems. U.S. President George Bush and Mexico President Carlos Salinas de Gortari initiated discussions between the countries to create a bilateral free trade association in order to promote economic recovery in Mexico and to reaffirm the trading relationships between the two nations. Canada, already associated through a free trade agreement, asked to participate in the negotiations between the United States and Mexico in the interest of developing a trilateral trade agreement that would create a common North American free trade zone with 360 million consumers and a $6 trillion market.

An agreement, worked out in negotiations over a period of years and widely debated in the media and legislative chambers, was approved by the three governments in 1993 and became operative on January 1, 1994. Basically, NAFTA sought to see that consumers bought more of their goods and services from within the region, that the three nations created the most efficient levels of productivity by using the strengths and resources of the partners, and that the region in concert seek to increase exports to other trading blocs or regional economies. In broad terms NAFTA proposed to eliminate trade barriers between the three nations over a period of 15 years, provide binding protection for the intellectual property rights of the region, and establish mechanisms for the settlement of disputes.

NAFTA specified that Mexico would reduce tariffs on automobiles from the United States and Canada by 10 percent immediately, eliminating the tariffs completely within ten years. Only autos certified as 62.5 percent North American manufactured would be entitled to the duty-free status. Mexico also would eliminate the requirement that American automobiles be manufactured in Mexico in order to be qualified for sale in Mexico. Trade and investment restrictions on energy and petrochemical firms in Mexico were to be lifted, and U.S. banks were to be allowed to open wholly owned subsidiaries in Mexico. Borders would be open to U.S. and Mexican cargo haulers—both ways. Imports from outside NAFTA would be subject to common tariff agreements and regulations. The agreement anticipated that NAFTA would divert American investments in manufacturing from Asia to Mexico, and that the United States would become a greater consumer of Mexican and Canadian products. Conversely, the agreements (from the American point of view) would deter Japanese and European investment and market penetration in North America. NAFTA, like the European Union and the Commonwealth of States, meant that traditional national economic autonomy was being subordinated in the interest of competing successfully with other global trading blocs.

Enthusiasm for such an agreement was not universal in Mexico, Canada, or the United States. Mexican and Canadian nationalist groups predicted the subordination of their country's national interests to the greater influence of the United States. Mexico's President Salinas, responding to concerns that the Mexican culture might be "Americanized," responded: "If you ask me if Mexicans will eat more hamburgers, my answer will be that Americans will eat more tacos." H. Ross Perot, a Texas businessman and presidential aspirant, predicted a "giant sucking sound" of American jobs being transferred to the lower-wage manufacturing industries to be located in Mexico. "The trade agreement will pit American and Mexican workers in a race to the bottom. In this race, millions of Americans will lose their jobs." The reality of U.S. companies transferring production to Mexico in order to take advantage of cheaper labor did in fact cause Congress to include funding for job retraining for those displaced by NAFTA. Agricultural producers in Texas predicted the flow of cheaper Mexican farm products across the border, resulting in recession for American farmers. Proponents predicted that increased North American trade would on the contrary create a net gain of 130,000 new jobs in the United States and that the more efficient allocation of resources in North America would make the NAFTA nations more competitive with other regional trading blocs.

Initial trade reports indicated that NAFTA was working as planned. The Department of Commerce reported that in the six months following approval of NAFTA, U.S. exports to Mexico had risen 17 percent over the levels of the previous year. The United States shipped $24.5 billion in goods to Mexico in the six-month period. Auto sales to Mexico tripled in the first five months of 1994 over the levels of the same period in 1993. U.S. exports to Canada rose by 10 percent to $55.6 billion. The United States also bought more goods and services from Mexico and Canada. Imports from Mexico to the United States ($23.4 billion) rose 21 percent over the previous period, and imports from Canada were up by 10 percent at $61.4 billion. Secretary of Commerce Ron Brown called it a "win-win-win" situation for all three countries.

U.S. exports of electronic materials rose sharply after the implementation of the NAFTA agreements. Digital integrated circuits, electronic integrated circuits, cathode ray tubes, computer parts, TV picture tubes, telephone parts, and even clothing exports to Mexico rose sharply in the first six months of 1994. Shipments of U.S. rolled steel products to Mexico rose from $58,000 to $26 million. The sale of jet engines to Mexico jumped from $13 million to $34 million. These were goods on which tariffs were completely eliminated between the countries. The nature of Mexico's purchases also suggested a fundamental reconstruction of Mexican business and manufacture into a higher-tech profile.

The Department of Commerce also noted, however, that in the same six-month period, the U.S. trade deficit with its two North American partners doubled from $478 million to $1 billion. The U.S. deficit with Japan rose 26 percent to $5.52 billion; the deficit with Europe climbed to $1.82 billion, and a trade deficit with China reached $2.46 billion. In the short run, at least, NAFTA was not having the desired impact on correcting the U.S. trade imbalance or North America's trade imbalance with the rest of the world.

Moreover, Americans doing business in Mexico and even Canada under the NAFTA accords faced considerable problems—problems that in many ways mirrored the task of conducting business on a global scale. Fishing and timber disputes with Canada, for example, continued to rankle businesses and leader on both sides of the border. Canadians and Mexicans were sensitive to the tendency of American business to dominate wherever it was being conducted. Conversely, Americans often misunderstood that which was being communicated by their counterparts in foreign countries. As one business executive explained, although Mexican businessmen may speak English, it did not mean that they did business in the same manner as did Americans. An American company, for example, competing to build a water purification plant in Mexico was astounded to be given the competitor's bid and invited to beat it. In the United States bid information is privileged. Payoffs to government officials was an accepted and often required way of doing business. Shipping delays and improper or incomplete documentation and records were chronic problems in Mexico. The solution, American firms began to discover, was to have trustworthy Mexican partners in across-the-borders business ventures. That seemed to be a good rule for the conduct of business anywhere outside the United States. Building those business bridges forged new links and stability in global commerce. International trade, even within North America, was a learning process.

An important part of the institutional structure affecting trade by NAFTA, the European Union, China, Japan, the Commonwealth of States, and those independent nations not formally affiliated with the world's great regional economies were the set of trading guidelines adopted by nations participating in the General Agreement on Tariffs and Trade (GATT).

GATT

A part of the post–World War II effort to maintain world peace and security involved an agreement entered into by twenty-three nations in 1947 to establish general guidelines or an understanding for the conduct of international trade and the imposition of tariffs. The idea was to remove barriers to world trade and provide a set of standards or rules by which nations established tariffs and trade regulations. Before World War II, and under the terms of America's own Reciprocal Trade Agreements Act of 1934, tariffs and trade agreements were always negotiated on a bilateral, nation-to-nation basis. Each nation had its own unique tariff schedules. Many, including the United States, used most-favored-nation standards to normalize trade between friendly nations or by withholding those standards to punish unfriendly traders. Most-favored-nation treatment meant that one nation would extend to the other the lowest tariff schedules granted to any other nation with whom the nation traded. The United States generally granted most-favored-nation treatment to all with whom it traded, but during the Cold War it did exclude certain nations (such as Cuba, North Korea, and the Soviet Union) from that standard.

The three basic principles were 1) the participating nations in GATT would all receive most-favored-nation treatment, and there would be no discrimination among them; 2) tariffs would be reduced through multilateral negotiations (not through bilateral agreements); and 3) import quotas would not be used by members other than to protect domestic agriculture or safeguard a nation's balance-of-payments position. These basic tenets were to produce a much more open and freer market. GATT also provided a mechanism for the review of complaints and trading problems.

Periodic reviews or rounds of negotiations followed the original agreements reached in 1947. What was called the Tokyo Round of multilateral trade negotiations began about 1974 and was concluded in 1979 when ninety-nine participating nations accepted the guidelines. Although tariffs had generally declined in the twenty years following the 1947 GATT agreements, nontariff barriers and impediments to trade had increased. Goods and services could be excluded from a country, for example, by imposing licensing conditions or by setting abnormally high valuations on a product so that while the tariff schedule may be uniformly low, the net tax resulted in excluding the product from the market. Product standards were also used to exclude foreign goods from a domestic market. Government procurement policies could also be discriminatory. The Tokyo Round adopted a code preventing or discouraging a government from discriminating against the products of foreign suppliers on contracts valued at $200,000 or more. The intensification of global trade in the 1980s led to fresh disagreements and a new Uruguay Round of negotiations that began in 1986.

The Uruguay Round examined more difficult and controversial issues affecting trade, including economic and public policies of the participating nations. Telecommunications, financial services, and tourism were service areas examined that had been previously overlooked in GATT negotiations. Patents, copyright, and trademark protection and infringement came under close examination. Agricultural policies and subsidies received special attention. European Union agricultural policies and subsidies resulted in the virtual exclusion of U.S. and foreign agricultural products from European markets. Scheduled for completion in 1990, Uruguay Round negotiations were not completed until 1993. The U.S. Congress approved the agreements on December 1, 1994. The European Union, Japan, and Canada did so in the months following.

The Uruguay Round was signed by 124 nations. The agreements reached would reduce global tariffs by approximately 40 percent — a major reduction. GATT was replaced through a phased transition by a new World Trade Organization that possessed stronger dispute-resolution capabilities. Reviews of trade disputes under the GATT organization could be vetoed by a GATT member. They could not be vetoed under the World Trade Organization. Tariffs were lowered in most areas and eliminated in some areas, as for beer, construction equipment, farm machinery, medical equipment, pharmaceuticals, and toys. The Uruguay Round provided seven years of protection for trademarks, twenty years for patents, and up to fifty years for copyrights. Electronics, computers, and computer software particularly benefited under the new agreements. Europe lowered its tariffs on computers from 4.9 percent to 2.5 percent, and the tariff on computer chips dropped by approximately one-half. Patents on computer hardware and medicines received special protection, as did copyrights on computer software.

Japan and South Korea lifted bans on rice imports that were particularly offensive to American rice producers. Audiovisuals, textiles, and financial services did not receive the treatment preferred by American producers. The United States, Europe, and Japan agreed to reduce tariffs further on textiles and clothing. That would reinforce the transfer of American textile manufacture to Mexico, India, and elsewhere, a process already underway. Inevitably, there were winners and losers in the multilateral trade agreements established under GATT processes, but the overall consensus was that all nations benefited. U.S. business leaders believed that the rounds concluded in 1994 would boost global business for years to come.

The GATT/World Trade Organization agreements provided a general code or guideline for the conduct of business among nations. By virtue of the multilateral nature of the agreements, confrontation between nations and between trading blocs was dissipated and diluted. GATT in other words provided a part of the adhesion or glue that bound the developing global economy into a cooperative and more stable, albeit competitive world. Because of the United Nations, GATT, and indeed the tone and policies established by the United States and its post–World War II trading and defense partners, although the world had become "regionalized," those regions might best be described as open or other-directed trading blocs rather than as insulated or isolated alliances more typical of the eighteenth and nineteenth centuries.

But the world had become less a community of nations or a community of individuals and more a community of regional economies. Although these regional economies and trading blocs were imperfect and fluid, failing to include a considerable number of the world's people, by the 1990s they set the tone and example for global trade and commerce. The European Union represented 500 million of the world's people, the Commonwealth of States approximately 500 million; NAFTA, 360 million; China, 1.2 billion; Japan and the Pacific Rim (including Burma, Indonesia, Thailand, the Philippines, Singapore, and Vietnam), 650 million; and OPEC (excluding the South American members), 140 million. These regional economic entities of Europe, CIS, NAFTA, OPEC, China, and Japan and the Pacific Rim constituted somewhat more than one-half of the world's population and accounted for as much as 90 percent of the world's product.

The Pacific Rim region obtained a firmer resolution in 1994 with the formation of an Asia Pacific Economic Cooperation group, supported by Japan, the United States, and China. The Pacific Rim nations agreed to work toward open regionalism. They pledged to work toward free and open trade throughout the region over the next twenty-five years, to create a tariff-free trade zone throughout Asia and the Pacific Rim, and to approve the GATT agreements. Japan and the United States agreed to eliminate their trade barriers by the year 2010, and China and South Korea, among others, would continue reductions through 2020.

South American republics, including Brazil, Argentina, Paraguay, Uruguay, Chile, and Bolivia have begun the inception of a common market or regional economy. Associating themselves in an organization called the Southern Cone Common Market (Mercosur), the new trade bloc in 1996 encompassed 210 million people with a domestic product of more than $900 million. Mercosur has scheduled a 40 percent tariff reduction between the trading partners beginning in October 1996, with the elimination of all duties by 2004.

The regional economies associated with one another through the United Nations and General Agreements on Tariffs and Trade, as well as through direct nation-to-nation and bloc-to-bloc agreements. NATO, for example, constituted a biregional defense and financial commitment. OPEC had market partners in South America. But corporate and personal associations, contracts, and agreements were the real substance of global trade and commerce between the regions.

Even in the 1990s not all of the world's peoples participated in global economic trade; not all participated in regional economic associations. India and South Asian nations constituted an unformed and unaligned geographic region of some 1.3 billion people. But for the Mediterranean states and South Africa, the African continent (500 million people) generally failed to participate in the developing global economy. There, as in the Balkans of Europe (Bosnia, Croatia, Serbia), tribalism undermined both nationalism and regionalism.

Nevertheless, what had come to be since the collapse of the communist system in the Soviet Union was a world largely committed to the idea that economic growth depended on free markets. A free market included clearly defined and transferable rights in private

The Globe's Regional Economies

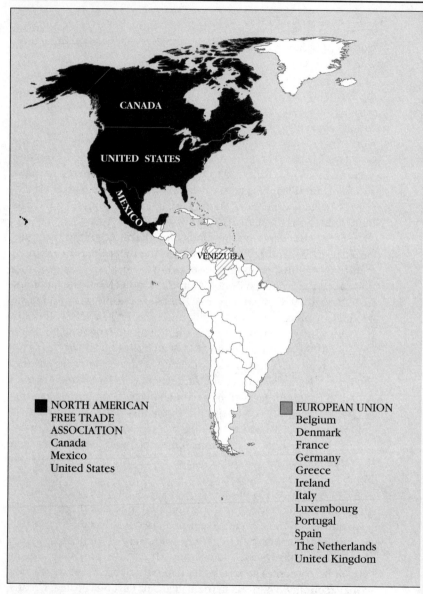

NORTH AMERICAN FREE TRADE ASSOCIATION
Canada
Mexico
United States

EUROPEAN UNION
Belgium
Denmark
France
Germany
Greece
Ireland
Italy
Luxembourg
Portugal
Spain
The Netherlands
United Kingdom

The globe's major trade associations or economic communities and unions are in various stages of development. All are relatively fluid, some amorphous. Independent associations often link individual members with nonaligned (or indirectly aligned) nations, thus most nations of the world are both directly and indirectly affected by the regional associations. Major trade blocs and associations include the European Union, the Commonwealth of Independent States, the North American

Free Trade Association, Japan and the Pacific Rim, OPEC, and China. China, a regional economic entity in its own right, is developing various associations with Pacific Rim nations (and beyond), and in 1997 annexed heavily capitalistic Hong Kong within its trade and political borders. Switzerland and Turkey (in particular) have established a remarkable degree of "interconnectedness" while maintaining considerable economic and political integrity.

property for peoples throughout the world. The creation and suste-
nance of open and free markets, it was believed, could best be
sought through multilateral trade agreements. The developing global
economy envisioned enforceable contracts within nations and
among nations. Global trade included accepting the principle of im-
partial adjudication of trade disputes. It meant accepting the idea
that change and growth were necessary parameters of human society. Humankind lived on the same planet Earth and had certain common interests and needs. While imperfect, possibly transient, and
always precarious, the Earth's peoples had taken a great step since
the close of World War II toward the creation of a true global
economy.

Chapter 10

THE NEW REALITY

The world has changed dramatically since 1945, and so has America's role in that world. American business was largely responsible for the Americanization of the global society. Even the Soviet Union and China, protected by iron and bamboo curtains, were vulnerable to Americanization and to the capitalist impulse it embodied. Americans espoused democracy, but were the purveyors of capitalism and materialism. But capitalism and democracy were not unrelated. Americanization of the global economy has had as much to do with establishing the worth of the individual, the protection of rights in private property, and in promoting free and open trade as it has with the sale of hamburgers, soft drinks, and blue denim pants. Through the Marshall Plan, foreign aid programs, and its global military presence, the United States established an unprecedented presence in the world in the half-century since World War II.

Following that war Europe and Japan performed, with American assistance, an economic miracle. Other regions of the world began to participate in the expanding business of the world. The OPEC nations moved from economic obscurity to world prominence and affluence. Asia and the Pacific Rim, almost belatedly, became a part of the global trading community. As the wealth, prosperity, and productivity of the world grew, America's position of dominance and economic hegemony declined relatively—but not absolutely. By 1970, the United States had entered a new phase of economic life.

Its business was no longer to Americanize the globe, but to globalize American business and economic institutions.

That proved to be unexpectedly difficult and painful. The United States became a debtor nation. Its trade imbalance grew. The federal debt rose. Business began a painful restructuring and reevaluation. New technologies, prominently electronics and computers, caused a shift in the character of American commerce. Communications and new technology began to supplant more traditional industries such as automobiles and defense. The United States began to restore its competitive edge by adopting new technology, through downsizing and streamlining corporate structures, through merger, and by forming multinational enterprises. The internal dynamics of American business began to change. The United States forged NAFTA, the North American Free Trade Association, and through multilateral negotiation worked to forge a more fair and open global marketplace for American business.

Globalization is a phenomenon that began and largely has been consummated since World War II. It has been consummated, but it really has not been fully assimilated in the public consciousness. Globalization is a process that has been contradictory to the American experience and traditions of separation, isolation, and independence. Globalism is, as Vaclav Havel suggested, also inconsistent with the more deep-rooted tendencies of humankind toward "chaos, disconnectedness and tribalism." The concept of a global economy refutes the historic development of the modern world as a world of independent, largely autonomous, nation-states. The nation-state and a national economy have been an intrinsic part of modern society since at least the seventeenth century. Nationalism emerged in part from the desire to create a political and social climate conducive to the development and protection of wealth. The nation-state received the financial and political support of the merchant and the developing middle class in return for order, the recognition of the worth of the individual, the protection of property rights, and the stability provided by the state.

Today, the interests of the merchant, the middle class, and the corporation extend to a larger global community. The multinational corporation, in particular, is less and less a thing identified with a nation and more and more a global or international entity. While rooted in the nation-state from which it springs, its stockholders and customers are dispersed around the globe. The constituency of the multinational corporation is a global constituency. Similarly, the marketplace has become a global marketplace. That global marketplace increasingly intrudes on how a person, wherever he or she dwells, lives and does business.

Adam Smith's laissez-faire capitalism argued that the best way for a nation to accumulate gold within the realm was to leave the individual to his or her own natural inclinations and instincts:

> As every individual . . . endeavors as much as he can to employ his capital in the support of domestic industry, and so to direct that industry that its produce may be of the greatest value, every individual necessarily labors to render the annual revenue of the society as great as he can.

That admonition holds true, but the society is now a larger, global society as opposed exclusively to a nation-state.

Today Americans and the burgeoning populations of the world are being challenged and coerced to accept the new reality of a global economy, to dilute the traditional and historic support of the nation-state, and to assume a new identity as citizens of a global community. The United Nations, NATO, GATT, technology, the Internet, the integration of financial markets, free trade agreements, and regional trade associations are among those factors erasing national borders and "uniting the world into a single, lucrative, but brutally competitive marketplace." Global integration creates winners and losers.

For the most part, the consensus is that the world's peoples have been winners. The per capita wealth of the world has risen significantly in the past fifty years. The world contains more than 5.5 billion people, twice that of fifty years ago, and it contains them for the most part in a better lifestyle than most obtained fifty years ago. Birth rates are generally higher except where controlled through contraceptive means and the law. Life spans are longer. Income is higher. But the world's wealth has by no means been evenly or unilaterally distributed. The contrast between the wealthy nations and the poorer ones has become greater. Older, secure, and established industries have been displaced or altered.

Globalism disturbs the existing order. The global revolution is in some respects equivalent to the advent of the industrial revolution. Industrialism resulted in the older, more simple, pastoral society being largely displaced. Symbolically, industrialism thrust the "machine" into the garden. Similarly, globalism intrudes on nationalism, provincialism, and tribalism and conflicts with past perceptions of what is good.

Just as industrialism set up mass migrations within a geographic area and the nation, as from the farm to the city, globalism has contributed to migration on a global scale. That has occurred because on the one hand the more advanced nations have offered opportunities for survival or material advancement in stark contrast to the underdeveloped countries. The contrast between the haves and the have-nots has stimulated migration.

Others have been displaced by war and economic dislocation rather than the incentive for new opportunities. A World Refugee Survey completed in 1987 estimated that 3.5 million Africans, 560,000 Asians (largely Vietnamese), 69,000 Europeans, 290,000 Latin Americans, and 8.8 million people from the Middle East and South Asia were refugees living in host countries. Open markets and open borders provided an open—but not always intended—invitation to outsiders to come in. Many of these migrants have been assimilated by the developed and developing nations who are in need of labor and human resources. But the migrants have also displaced many of those already employed. Workers in a host country often fear dispossession and unemployment forced by the migration of workers from elsewhere. India has begun the construction of the world's longest fence to block immigrants from Bangladesh. More than one million people a year legally immigrate to the United States, and many have come without permission. The United States has constructed barriers to deter illegal immigrants from Mexico on the one hand, while transferring manufactures to Mexico and advocating free trade and open markets with Mexico under the NAFTA accords on the other hand. France, England, and Germany have faced rising social unrest centering on the growing migrant groups settling among existing communities. Migrants from the turbulent Middle East have presented a continuing social and political problem for host countries. The dispossessed of Africa have themselves suffered, but have also caused health problems and hardship on host countries. Starvation and epidemics have often followed mass migrations. Global migration has been an unsettling process.

The globalization of the world has on the one hand contributed to greater migration, but it has also provided structures and opportunities (and the obligation) to care for the migrants. Thus, the

United Nations and the United States have assisted in providing food and shelter for Somalia's famine and for the refugees of the Hutu and Tutsi wars in Central Africa. James Wolfenshon, president of the World Bank, has called upon governments to raise $1.2 billion for the reconstruction of Bosnia and the employment of the 250,000 fighting men being demobilized after the long and bitter internecine wars. He estimated that $5.1 billion will be needed over a three-year period to help restore stability in the region and to deter what could become another mass migration.

Migration (immigration) has created social stress within many nations, including the United States. It has incited the old tribalism, racism, and nationalism. By the interdiction of diverse religions and philosophies, migration threatens perceived order and stability. Migrants compete with domestic labor for jobs. And migration is—not wholly but at least in part—a product of globalism. Because it has seemingly fostered migration and resulted in theocratic and philosophical challenges to the existing order, whatever they may be, the rise of globalism has induced a reaction.

The global marketplace itself, like migration, also tends to stir reaction. Traditional buyers and sellers have changed. They are more different and diverse. They speak different languages and assign different values to goods and services than have been customary and traditional in the local marketplace. Competition is intense and more impersonal. A merchant may well long to return to the old way of doing business as an opportunity to reestablish an advantage formerly enjoyed but now lost. Employees and even manufacturers may advocate protective tariffs to deter competition and sustain existing employment conditions.

Reaction to globalism has indeed taken many forms. The hardliner coup and attempted overthrow of Mikhail Gorbachev in the Soviet Union, the Tianenmen Square riots and massacre in Beijing, China, riots in England, France, and Germany, building fences in India and the United States, the rise of the old isolationist and fundamentalist impulses in the United States, and growing terrorist attacks are all evidence of social unrest and change. There are those who doubt that globalism can survive the inevitable reaction.

The development of a global economy has altered, among other things, the nature of the American governing system. The United States has perhaps politically and economically ''Americanized'' the world, but the United States is also adjusting and altering its business, social, and political institutions to fit the new global order.

The American presidency, for example, has become increasingly an office for global interaction more than for domestic policy making. Since Harry Truman's administration there has been a distinct tilt toward foreign affairs. During his four years in office President George Bush made twenty-five international journeys. Those trips included visits with heads of state, economic summits, good-will tours, trade talks, a drug summit, a state funeral, and visits to American troops stationed overseas. Most trips had to do with trade and commerce. President Bill Clinton has followed a similar pattern of international travel. In April 1995 alone, President Clinton met in South Korea with South Korean President Kim Young Sam, in Japan with Prime Minister Ryutaro Hashimoto, and in Moscow with Russian President Boris Yeltsin. Through most of its history American presidents were not expected to leave American soil. Now, the American president is regarded as the American emissary to the world.

Globalism has affected the world's language and communications. English has become an almost universal second language. It is to the globe what Latin was to the Mediterranean world 2000 years ago. Real-time global communications have also been made possible by virtue of communications satellites placed in orbit about the Earth. People can not only talk to each other or see each other from almost any point on the Earth, they can now view their planet from space. They have become, thus, "Earth people" rather than Russians, Americans, and people of other nations. The view of the planet does not denote national boundaries. Earth has become, compared to what it once was, a "small, small world." Improved communications and universal language skills have facilitated the growth of the global economy and the global village.

American business, and the way American business conducts its business has changed. Business for one thing is bigger. It is global. Economic assistance to less developed countries by Western governments and the United States helps provide the infrastructure for business investment and market expansion to follow. American, Japanese, and European firms have established new alliances and associations through buy-outs and acquisitions. The opening of markets and new sources of labor and competition on a global scale have contributed to the relocation of manufactures. Mexico, China, and Russia in particular have become targets for Western capital investment and business expansion. Capital investment and economic assistance programs, not coincidentally, relieve areas of economic distress, lessen the migration and uprooting of populations, and reduce global tensions.

In recent years American business has restructured itself to better meet global competition. It has become leaner and more streamlined and efficient. In the process employees have lost their jobs and those employed are doing much more than in the past. Premiums have been placed on technology and the quality of human resources. The goal is more efficient production, a better profit margin, and survival. Since the 1980s American business has become more competitive in the global marketplace.

Among the world's one hundred largest corporations in 1995, forty-one were American, thirty-seven Japanese, and twenty-one European/United Kingdom, and one based in Singapore. The world's largest corporation, by value of its stock, was Nippon Telephone and Telegraph (NTT), followed by Royal Dutch/Shell. The United States listed General Electric, AT&T, and Exxon among the world's ten largest corporations. Among the one hundred largest banks, twenty-nine were Japanese, thirty-one European Union, and nine U.S. In 1995, the United States and North America held approximately 8 percent of the world's population, Europe and the United Kingdom 14 percent, and Asia (including Japan) 60 percent. Mainland China, with 1.4 billion people, had almost 25 percent of the world's total population. Europe had about 500 million people, Russia and the Commonwealth of Independent States 300 million, the United States and NAFTA 300 million, and Japan (125 million) and Pacific Rim nations (including primarily Burma, Indonesia, the Philippines, Thailand, and Vietnam) accounted for 2 billion people. For the most part most of the world's population have only in recent years been exposed to the global economy.

The collapse of communism in the former Soviet Union and the greater access to China profoundly and positively affected the development of the global economy. The United States and a good portion of the world from 1945 through 1990 were preoccupied with the Cold War rather than with world commerce and trade. During the Cold War the issues seemed clear and incontrovertible. The issue was, who was for us, and who was against us? How could American resources best be used to defend the United States and the free world from the threat of nuclear war or engage in a land war in Europe? The end of the Cold War has diffused the issues and multiplied choices. The new post–Cold War global economy presented the United States with unparalleled opportunities and with new problems.

Much of the world, primarily the former Soviet Union, experienced chaos and confusion. Conversion to capitalism and democracy has not been easy or painless. Danger and violence, "tribalism and disconnectedness" are always imminent. The 1990s is a particularly critical decade in the transition to democracy, capitalism, and globalism. In 1993, Vaclav Havel's Czechoslovakia divided peaceably into two separate republics, the Czech Republic and the Republic of Slovakia. After an initial spate of democracy and capitalism, Russia and many of its former satellite republics turned to former communist leaders and administrators to replace the democrats and reformers initially chosen to head the new independent governments. Poland's electorate, for example, elected Lech Walesa its first noncommunist premier in December 1990. Walesa began the process of transforming Poland to a free market economy. In 1993, voters retired Walesa and selected a coalition of communists to power. Poland hung precariously between a free market and a return to a controlled market.

Poland, Russia, and Hungary turned even more to former communist leaders and officials in elections held in 1994 and 1995. In 1996, Russia's President Boris Yeltsin sought reelection in a hotly disputed race with presidential candidate and leader of the communist party, Gennadi A. Zyuganov, who married "resentful, xenophobic strains of nationalism with crowd-pleasing themes of Soviet nostalgia, historical revisionism and old-fashioned socialism." The elections in the former Soviet countries echoed across the ocean.

Despite the distances and apparent disparities, attitudes and events in Russia mirrored to an extent conditions in the United States where a growing post–Cold War contingency in the U.S. Congress advocated withdrawal from NATO, abandonment of the United Nations, an end to U.S. foreign aid, and reduction of foreign expenditures. In Russia the election of former communists represented less a return to radicalism and more an attempt to cling to stability and order such as it had existed for the past fifty years. In the United States a return to isolation, nationalism, and disengagement appeared an attractive alternative to globalism and the changes implicit with the global community. Capitalism in the Soviet Union, as did globalism in the United States meant change, chaos, and confusion. Holding steadily to the past, whatever that past may have been, offered to some in those countries at least a sense of stability and order.

Similarly, the European Union, struggling to meet its objectives for a unified currency discovered that currencies not only serve as a medium for commerce and exchange, but symbolize the integrity and viability of the nation-state. Can there be a Germany without the Deutsche Mark or a France without the Franc? Creating a single market in Europe confronts not only vested interests, but also national pride, local customs, diverse business and labor practices, and a plethora of often conflicting laws. Many in Europe do not think that real market consolidation is possible. But the alternatives are disconnectedness and the impairment of trade and commerce. The question of a unified currency alone brings into focus the present reality of the nation-state on the one hand and the new global reality on the other.

Are members of the European Union better served with a common currency or separate currencies? In 1995 there were twelve members of the European Union, each with its own national currency. Austria joined in 1995. Prospective members included Finland, Norway, Sweden, Hungary, Poland, and the Czech Republic. Can an economic union survive twelve or fifteen different currencies each with a different relative value? The question is not wholly academic. In 1995, an American tourist or business person, for example, who flew to Paris and traveled from there to Germany for a pleasure or business trip among the Danube countries had to convert the dollar variously to the franc, mark, kronen (Slovakia), schilling (Austria), and forint (Hungary). Each exchange of currency exacts a toll of as much as 5 percent of the total. A visitor to five countries can theoretically lose as much as 25 percent of his or her purchasing power simply exchanging currencies. A confusion of value-added taxes (VATs) adds to the problem of purchasing and transferring goods across national boundaries.

Currency exchanges and disparate taxes reduce direct expenditures and discourage spending on goods and services. Not only is there a loss of investment or purchasing dollar due to money exchange costs, but also the buyer is necessarily deterred by having to deal in currencies with varying values related to the dollar. In spring 1995, for example, the U.S. dollar purchased 5 French francs, 1.5 German marks, 30 Slovakian kronen, 20 Austrian schillings, and 140 Hungarian forints. Those rates varied (at least in theory) day by day. A uniform currency, while undermining national autonomy, encourages trade and commerce and promotes the competitiveness of the European Union. But it might also reasonably be expected to undermine the historic sense of national and cultural identity of the participating nations.

While Europe grapples with these more sophisticated problems of an advanced economic union, China, only recently off-limits to capitalism and change, now seeks to use capitalism without becoming

capitalistic. The future of Hong Kong, the Pacific Rim's most capitalistic, democratic, and productive region, as it enters under Chinese
control and authority tests to an extent the new flexibility and open-
ness of China, and indeed, the viability of the global economy. China
contains the world's single largest developing market. The market
for aircraft in China is estimated at $100 billion over the next two
decades. The United States and France are currently competing intensely for entry into that market. The potential market in China for
communications systems, medicine, automobiles, and computers is
enormous. Mainland China has enjoyed the highest growth rate in
the world in the past twelve years. With that growth and with China's "opening" have come dissidence and factionalism within China
as there has been in the West.

Smaller and less-developed countries are still on the fringe of the
global economy. Many countries, to be sure, have yet to be introduced to the global economy. Others have only a marginal involvement. Some lack the stability and infrastructure to become viable
elements of the global community. Some nations, geographically sep-
arated as are South Africa, Australia, and New Zealand, are substan-
tially integrated into the European market system. India, while
independent, has close and historical trade relations with the United
Kingdom and Southeast Asia. With a history of democracy and capitalism, India has enormous potential that is more susceptible to development in the rising global economy than in the colonialism of its
recent past. Latin American nations in particular are developing access to capital and more stable political systems. All areas of the
world are more susceptible to change today than they were half a
century ago because of the omnipresence of the global economy.

The global economy is developing as a cluster of federated regional economies that has somewhat subordinated national interests
of the member states to the greater interests of the region. The federated regional economies include North America, the European
Union, Japan and the Pacific Rim, Russia and the Commonwealth of
Independent States, China, and OPEC. Competition between regions
and trading blocs is intense. Within the global economic regions,
competition and rivalry among the nations comprising the various
regional federations is keen but controlled. Globally, the United
Nations, GATT, self-interest, and simple survival mediate the excesses
of regional rivalries. Nations continue to exist within the regions as
do provinces and states, tribes, enclaves, cities, and communities,

each with their own autonomy and interests. Those nations and peoples exist as they always have, but they are being sublimated and subjected to a new reality. The world's adjustment to the new reality of a global economy is a process just beginning.

BIBLIOGRAPHY

U.S. Government Documents are particularly useful sources for inquiry into American foreign trade and the global economy. A sense of the immediacy and reality of the global economy can be realized simply by viewing reports relating to International Transactions and Foreign Aid, Foreign Commerce, and Export and Import tables in the U.S. Census reports. The *Historical Statistics of the United States* are recommended.

A rich resource for inquiries into foreign trade and the U.S. position in the global economy are the U.S. Department of Agriculture, Economic Research Service—National Agricultural Statistics Service (ERS-NASS) reports. The Situation and Outlook Series of the *International Agriculture and Trade Reports* provide both a macro and micro insight into aspects of world trade and commerce. There are annual and special situation reports on China, the Western Hemisphere, Western Europe, Russia, Asia and the Pacific Rim, Latin America, Mexico, and Canada to mention a few. ERS-NASS also produces General Agreements of Tariffs and Trade (GATT) and World Trade Organization (WTO) reports, global reviews of agricultural policy, reports on the impact of environmental policies on global trade, trends and indicators affecting world agriculture, and numerous special reports.

Other documentary resources include the *United Nations (UN) Statistical Yearbook* and the *UN Demographic Yearbook,* as well as other special UN reports. The North Atlantic Treaty Organization (NATO), Food and Agricultural Organization (FAO), International Monetary Fund (IMF), and Organization of American States (OAS) issue annual and special reports—many of them quite useful for examining the development of the global economy.

Government documents that targeted the problems of a developing global economy since 1945 that were particularly useful to the author included Peter G. Peterson, *A Foreign Economic Perspective* (GPO: Council on International Economic Policy), December 27, 1971, vol. 1, and Peterson, *The United States in the Changing World Economy* (GPO: Council on International Economic Policy), December 27, 1971, vol. 2. I would recommend for an overview of the United States in the context of global trade and competition the Report on the President's Commission on Industrial Competitiveness, *Global Competition: The New Reality* (GPO: January 1985), 2 vols. It offers a good analysis of the situation.

Texts on international economics are handy for a preliminary orientation to the problems and concepts of foreign trade and a global economy. There are many such texts available, but the author has found Robert J. Carbaugh, *International Economics* (Cincinnati, Ohio: International Thomson Publishing, 1995), and Dale W. Jornenson, vol. 1, *Postwar U.S. Economic Growth* and vol. 2, *Productivity: International Comparisons of Economic Growth* (Cambridge, Mass.: The MIT Press, 1995) helpful. And see John Charles Pool and Steve Stamos, *The ABCs of International Finance* (Lexington, Mass.: D. C. Heath, 1987), and Christine Rider, *Introduction to Economic History* (Cincinnati, Ohio: International Thomson Publishing, 1995) (very little on economy since 1945, but useful background and general orientation).

For overviews of American business history see Keith L. Bryant, Jr., and Henry C. Dethloff, *A History of American Business,* 2d ed. (Prentice-Hall, 1990), or Henry C. Dethloff and C. Joseph Pusateri, *American Business History: Case Studies* (Harlan Davidson, 1987). The table for Union Carbide's international branches used in Chapter 8 derives from a case study authored by Jimmy Anklesaria in the preceding text.

A wealth of information and data are available in the University Publications of America, microfiche *Documentary Case Studies in International Trade,* the *International Trade: Special Studies Series* (1971-1985), and *Multinational Corporations* microfilm series

(1971–1985). The *Japan-U.S. Semiconductor Cases* offers a classic study in international trade policy nuances and negotiations.

A diplomatic history text also offers good insight into the developing global economy. Stephen E. Ambrose, *Rise to Globalism: American Foreign Policy since 1938,* 5th rev. ed. (New York: Viking Penguin Books, 1988) provides a good overview. Walter LeFeber, *The New Empire* (Ithaca: Cornell University Press, 1963); Ernest R. May, *Imperial Democracy* (New York: Harcourt, Brace & World, 1961); and Charles S. Campbell, Jr., *Special Business Interests and the Open Door Policy* (New Haven: Yale University Press, 1951) focus on the role of big business in the creation of American imperialism. They reflect what might be termed the traditional view that doing business abroad often leads to bad things. It might be noteworthy that American diplomatic history texts treat diplomacy as an extension of American policy abroad. Diplomatic history has not really focused on the developing economics of a global community. Is there a developing *global* diplomacy, or world policy? That would, of course, change the traditional perception of what diplomacy is all about.

Several broadly constructed and interpretive books that bear on the question of globalism and the American presence or position in the global economy include Ira C. Magaziner and Robert B. Reich, *Minding America's Business: The Decline and Rise of the American Economy* (New York: Random House, 1982). That excellent and focused work admonishes Americans to "acknowledge that the nation is dependent on a dynamic world economy that must be better understood."

Books that your author regards as very relevant to America's role in a dynamic world economy include David M. Potter, *People of Plenty: Economic Abundance and the American Character* (Chicago: University of Chicago Press, 1954). In a somewhat similar vein, and full of interesting ideas about American business and society, see Louis Galambos, *America at Middle Age: A New History of the U.S. in the Twentieth Century* (New York: McGraw-Hill, n.d.).

The historical literature of the early post–World War II years focused on the problems of demobilization and disarmament, and then in very short order, on the problem of rearming and sustaining a permanent defense posture. There are, of course, many books about the Cold War. Relatively few, however, truly focus on global trade and commerce or on the impact of defense spending on the global economy. The economic impact of defense spending and more recently the economics of demobilization are subjects of considerable interest because of the collapse of the Soviet Union and the presumed end of the Cold War.

Some useful titles on the subject of defense spending are William L. Baldwin, *The Structure of the Defense Market, 1955–1964* (Durham: Duke University Press, 1967), and Seymour Melman, *Pentagon Capitalism: The Political Economy of the Cold War* (New York: McGraw-Hill Book Company, 1970). Melman is a strong critic of the "military industrial complex" and a prolific author. See also his *The Defense Economy: Conversion of Industries and Occupations to Civilian Needs* (New York: Praeger Publishers, 1970). A useful overview of key issues involved is offered in James L. Clayton, ed., *The Economic Impact of the Cold War: Sources and Readings* (New York: Harcourt, Brace & World, Inc., 1970). The more recent John E. Lynch, ed., *Economic Adjustment and Conversion of Defense Industries* (Boulder, Colo.: Westview Press, 1987), provides a more contemporary view, as does David Gold, *The Impact of Defense Spending on Investment, Productivity and Economic Growth* (Washington, D.C.: Defense Budget Project, February 1990).

Business history, understandably, has for the most part focused on the firm and how the firm operates within the context of the American marketplace. That is a testament to the problems related to the rise of a global economy, that is, American firms and American policy makers despite international involvement have retained a largely provincial or domestic view of the world. That is likely to change, both for business and for the business historian.

Recommended titles that effectively treat the global dimensions of American business include John Strohmeyer's Pulitzer prize–winning *Crisis in Bethlehem: Big Steel's Struggle to Survive* (New York: Viking Penguin Books, 1987). Although it has a domestic focus, the theme in Frederick Lewis Allen's *Secret Formula: How Brilliant Marketing and Relentless Salesmanship Made Coca-Cola the Best-Known Product in the World* (New York: HarperCollins, 1994) is a global one. J. C. Louis and Harvey Z. Yazijian, *The Cola Wars* (New York: Everest House, 1980), and Robert Sobel, *IBM: Colossus in Transition* (New York: Time Books, 1981), focus on the domestic scene but contain global references.

The best business histories with global connotations have been in oil and OPEC. The titles are many and often quite good. See, for example, Irvine H. Anderson, *Aramco, The United States and Saudi Arabia: A Study of the Dynamics of Foreign Oil Policy, 1933–1950* (Princeton: Princeton University Press, 1981), or Charles W.

Hamilton, *Americans and Oil in the Middle East* (Houston: Gulf Publishing Company, 1962). George Ward Stocking's *Middle East Oil: A Study in Political and Economic Controversy* (Memphis: Vanderbilt University Press, 1970) is highly recommended. Irvine H. Anderson's, *Aramco, The United States and Saudi Arabia: A Study of the Dynamics of Foreign Oil Policy, 1933-1950,* previously mentioned, offers a good background for Stocking's later analyses. Both of these stop short of the OPEC embargo. An oil man of a different stripe was Armand Hammer. Steve Weinberg's *Armand Hammer: The Untold Story* (Boston: Little, Brown, 1989) is a fascinating account.

The computer and microchip books are just beginning to come online. As true with business history generally, studies of the computer and electronic industries are most often focused on the domestic U.S. scene. But the subject is laden with global relevance. In addition to the IBM study mentioned previously, see, for example, Stuart M. DeLuca, *Television's Transformation: The Next 25 Years* (New York: A. S. Barnes & Company, 1980), and Joel Shurkin, *Engines of the Mind: History of the Computer* (W. W. Norton & Company, 1984). Shurkin's book, published in 1984, essentially ends where the PC begins. For the Silicon Valley–PC story beginnings, see Paul Freiberger and Michael Swaine, *Fire in the Valley: The Making of the Personal Computer* (Berkeley, Calif.: Osborne/McGraw-Hill, 1984). One suspects that a ripe field for international business history will be in the harvest of PC firm stories. Industrial espionage (particularly relating to the computer industry) will be a theme worth pursuing.

Because Japan has become a major trading partner of the United States, and its economy has become one of the major factors in world trade, your author recommends some attention to Japan beginning with Dan Fenno Henderson, ed., *The Constitution of Japan, Its First Twenty Years, 1947-1967* (Seattle: University of Washington Press, 1968), and Mitsuaki Okabe, ed., *The Structure of the Japanese Economy* (New York: St. Martin's Press, 1995). And see, too, Thomas K. McCraw, ed., *America versus Japan: A Comparative Study* (Boston: Harvard Business School Press, 1986); Jerome B. Cohen, ed., *Pacific Partnership: U.S.-Japan Trade* (Lexington: Japan Society, Inc., 1972); and James Rader, *Penetrating the U.S. Auto Market: German and Japanese Strategies, 1965-1976* (Ann Arbor: University of Michigan Research Press, 1980). Also pertinent is Eric J. Toder, *Trade Policy and the U.S. Auto Industry* (New York: Praeger, 1978).

While it is not bibliography, a real learning experience in global trade and commerce is an extended visit to Japan, Hong Kong, and other cities in Southeast Asia and the Pacific Rim. The opening of the China market is something yet to be proven and studied, but for starters try Jonathan R. Woetzel, *China's Economic Opening to the Outside World* (New York: Praeger, 1989). The fact that America's trade imbalance with China grew sharply in 1995–1996 is indicative of the accelerating trade developing between the two countries. Trade between the two was almost nonexistent even in 1990.

Multinational corporations are receiving more recognition and treatment in the literature. Ground-breaking studies are Mira Wilkins, *The Emergence of Multinational Enterprise: American Business Abroad from the Colonial Era to 1914* (Cambridge: Harvard University Press, 1970) and *The Maturing of Multinational Enterprise: American Business Abroad from 1914 to 1970* (Cambridge: Harvard University Press, 1974). Fred V. Carstensen's *American Enterprise in Foreign Markets: Singer and International Harvester in Imperial Russia* (Chapel Hill: University of North Carolina Press, 1984) is a good model for MNC history. There is much more that needs to be done.

Given the recent rise of globalism and the development of a global economy it is likely that international business history, studies of the multinational corporation, and economic history from the global perspective will occupy an increasingly larger place in the literature.

CREDITS

INDEX